I0155189

Broken Hearts

"Scripture taken from the New King James Version. Copyright © 1982 by Thomas Nelson, Inc.

Copyright © 2019 Summer McClellan

All rights reserved. This book or any portion thereof may not be reproduced or used in any manner whatsoever without the express written permission of the publisher except for the use of brief quotations in a book review.

ISBN:978-1-950252-10-7

Broken Hearts

Hope for the Hurting

By Summer McClellan

To: *Paul*

Contents

Introduction

This book was inspired by a young man named Paul. I hardly knew him, I only met him once, but he was on my prayer list. He was a friend of my niece, Missy. My niece is also on my prayer list. She has had a battle with depression. She attempted suicide at fifteen and has been floundering ever since, not only with her mental health but also with her faith.

My beautiful niece. It is hard for me to understand what the problem is. She is so lovely I have to stare at her when I see her. She is so feminine and so sweet that you just want to be near her. She has an artistic flair also and she creates beauty. She makes beautiful things; she is an artist.

I remember I was over at my sister's one day and Missy was making a plant arrangement. She had bought several plants and she arranged them together in a different container. I couldn't believe how lovely it looked. I sat there amazed at her flair for beauty.

So, it is hard for me to understand why she has a problem. Several times she has checked herself into the hospital for mental help.

One thing that really has helped Missy is her little dog named Pablo. We never even knew how much she loved animals until Pablo. Pablo became her baby. I have never been too fond of dogs but even I love Pablo, he is a friendly little lap dog who loves everyone but especially Missy.

Missy was anxious to get her own place, she is in her twenties, and wanted to get out on her own. She met Paul online. Paul lived in a town about an hour and a half away and rented a small mobile home. He offered to sublet his mobile home with Missy. We of course were concerned about the whole situation, but that is not what this story is about, it is about Paul.

My sister, Carol kept me informed about what was going on when we met each week to pray. We soon added Paul to our prayer list. We decided he was part of the family.

We found out more about Paul. Paul, who was only a couple years older than Missy, was also suffering mentally. He had post-traumatic stress disorder after serving overseas. He also had never known his mom until recently and had a traumatic childhood.

Paul was barely existing. He had a factory job, he worked, came home and ate a tv dinner and slept or watched television until he worked again.

In comes Missy with color and beauty, hanging curtains and fixing real meals. Not just Missy but also Pablo. Pablo loved Paul so much also, that he was torn between the two of them, and he slept in the hall between Paul's room and Missy's room, so he could keep an eye on both of them.

I wanted to meet Paul, I don't know why but I cared about him from the moment I heard about him. I got my chance. He came with Missy to a birthday party for my mother which was at my house. Paul and Missy came in with Pablo like two new parents. He was big, burly, and handsome. I could tell he was very nervous and uncomfortable around people. That was the only time I saw him. I was secretly hoping Paul and Missy's story would end like my husband and I, two broken people meeting each other's needs.

Paul was in love with Missy and Pablo, and he wanted a life. But Paul was too broken to allow himself any happiness. And even though Missy was happy with her new situation, Paul went into rages if Missy went anywhere. Also, he suffered from depression and stayed in bed for days, and at other times he had mood swings. He would panic when they tried to go places and demand to go home. Later when he seemed more like himself, he always apologized. Several times when Paul went into a rage Missy came back home to her mom's but then returned to Paul as soon as he calmed down.

There were peaceful times. One day Missy and Paul watched a Christian program on television, called, *It's Supernatural*. Paul was enthralled. They talked about speaking in tongues and healing. Paul couldn't get enough of it and watched episode after episode. He prayed for healing at the end of the show. When Carol and I heard about this we were thrilled. We hoped Paul could be normal.

Paul knew he was broken but he could not pull himself together. Paul was so torn up inside he went to pieces. Finally, after several months Missy had to leave because she felt she was in danger. Paul threatened to kill himself, but she left anyway. I was surprised Missy stayed away but I knew she was thinking it was best for Paul. Because he was so torn up about his feelings for her, she thought staying away would be best.

Missy got a call from Paul's landlord that he was in the hospital. She wanted to see him, but she didn't want to stir things up again, so she didn't. Several weeks later Missy found out Paul had died. We think it was from sepsis. He had infection and was put into a coma to have his leg amputated but he never came out of it. Missy was devastated.

Not only Missy, Carol and I were too.

I grieved for Paul, a young man only in his twenties that never even had a chance at life. He fell through the cracks, of life. It was tragic. Reading his obituary only made it worse. There were only a couple of lines. There was only one comment written in memorial, only one.

I could not get rid of the grief. In desperation, I implored the Lord to tell me if Paul was with Him.

Silence.

I prayed harder.

Silence.

I determined to pray until I knew. I had a suspicion that Paul was with the Lord, but I needed to know! I wondered why the Lord refused to answer.

I woke up in the middle of the night. And I knew why the Lord wouldn't answer me. His word to me was this. *"I have called you to the Paul's of this world, the heartbroken. I want you to remember Paul and I want your heart to remain tender. You will always have that doubt, maybe Paul is lost forever. I am going to leave you wondering so your heart will remain tender to those who are like Paul, the broken hearted."*

This book is dedicated to Paul, a young man in great pain who seemingly lived and died unnoticed, and to those like Paul, the broken hearted.

Chapter One

The Heart of the Matter

Keep your heart with all diligence, For out of it spring the issues of life. Proverbs 4:23

You have heard the phrase the heart of the matter. If we say that, we mean, the center of the matter the most important thing. Our heart is our center. It is the core of our being and who and what we are. Our heart is more than just an organ that pumps our blood. That is our physical heart and that is a vital organ. It pumps life to our body and without it; of course, we would die immediately. Our physical heart is vital to keeping our body alive and keeping us here in the physical plane.

But we are more than just a body, we are also a living soul and spirit. We are a tri-part being. Our spirit also has organs and functions. It is not just a ghostly thing. Our spirit has organs and senses just like our body which gives us function on the spiritual plane just as our body does on the physical plane.

Our spiritual functions, which we can walk in, are considered supernatural by most. Our spirit can function in amazing ways and if you want to know what they are, then look at the life of our Lord, Jesus. He came to earth and functioned as a functional tri-part being. And through Him we can become the same. We become naturally supernatural.

We also have a soul. Our soul is a necessary part of our being which acts between our spirit and our body. All three parts of our being have a heart which are connected together, and that is the center of our being, they operate together. I know this is true, I can feel it.

There have been many times in my life {in everyone's life} when I have been in deep distress. I literally feel pain in my heart. I know I don't have to rush to the hospital because of the pain, although I physically feel it, because it is coming from my spirit and my soul, but I feel it in my physical heart also. They are connected together.

Our being, spirit soul and body, is connected together by what the scripture calls the silver cord, which when it is broken our body will die.

Remember your Creator before the silver cord is loosed, Or the golden bowl is broken, Or the pitcher shattered at the fountain, Or the wheel broken at the well. Then the dust will return to the earth as it was, And the spirit will return to God who gave it. Ecclesiastes 12:1

Our Born Again Spirit

I am talking about our spirit as though it were born again. But before we are born again our being is not in proper order. Something is terribly wrong. Because of sin entering the human race our tri-part being is not working. Even before we sin, we are affected by sin. We are born into a fallen state that began with Adam's sin. In fact, all three parts of us are affected by sin.

Therefore, just as through one man sin entered the world, and death through sin, and thus death spread to all men, because all sinned. Romans 5:12

In our fallen state we are doomed. We also do not function as we were created. Our spirit does not have access to the spirit realm and fellowship with God. It is fallen. Our body is subject to death and our minds are not renewed.

Salvation is more than just a new state of mind. It is an actual change in our being. The Spirit of God literally joins with our spirit; Jesus really does come into our heart. In the anatomy of your spirit there is literally a place where the spirit of God comes in and lives.

I believe He occupies the area above my belly button up to my heart. I believe this because I can feel Him there. I feel life and power there. Let's look at a few scriptures. *But he who is joined to the Lord is one spirit with Him. Or do you not know that your body is the temple of the Holy Spirit who is in you, whom you have from God, and you are not your own? 1 Corinthians 6:17 and 19*

He that believeth on Me, as scripture has said, out of his belly shall flow rivers of living water John 7:38

Our Mind

Our mind is not our center, although our mind is also important. When I say our mind, I am also talking about the brain and the reasoning part of our soul. We should not be ruled by our mind.

My mind is usually a hindrance to my spirit. I can't tell you how many times my mind has messed up my instructions from my heart. I will give you a little example. Last year I got an e-mail from my heating company offering a furnace repair service, for a small fee added onto the bill. My spirit prompted me to sign up for it. Before I did my mind got a hold of it and reasoned that my furnace was new and should not need repair and that fee would add up, so I didn't do it.

Well, my mind is natural, but my spirit is supernatural because it is connected to God's Spirit, and my spirit knew what was coming. My furnace broke down several times that year and the huge repairs depleted my finances, had I listened to my spirit and not my mind I would have saved myself a lot of trouble and money.

Now there have been times that I have listened also, many times. One time I was driving and for no apparent reason I felt too slow way down, which I did, when suddenly a deer ran in front of my car which I was easily able to miss because I listened to my heart. These things are daily occurrences. We need to listen to our spirit man which comes from the center of our being and not our mind. Our spirit man is in contact with God. Our mind, though necessary, will only offer us reason while our spirit man has supernatural insight.

Trust in the Lord with all your heart and lean not on your own understanding; In all your ways acknowledge Him, And He shall direct your paths Proverbs 3:5

So our minds were never intended to be the

ruling place in our lives. Our minds are not the part of us in contact with God, our spirit is.

Broken Hearts

Because of sin in all of us who come from Adam, {all of us,] we are all born with a level of damage, and depending on our lives, from there on we may receive more damage. Some have more damage than others. We are damaged in all three levels of our tri-part being, our spirits our souls and our bodies. Sin and brokenness are passed down in our DNA.

Some family lines have greater measure of sin in them than others, and the children born into them have more stacked against them than others before they even begin their lives. Some are born with hardly a chance in life at all; they are born into brokenness and to very broken people and will immediately suffer even more. They are born with more problems than others. Some don't even seem better after they become a Christian, they are just too broken. Some live and die broken hearted lives with no relief whatsoever.

Is this fair? Are they doomed from the beginning? Is God still a just God to allow this to happen? Is there any hope at all?

Chapter Two

Created in God's Image

*Then God said, "Let Us make man in Our image,
according to Our likeness; let them have dominion over the
fish of the sea, over the birds of the air, and over the cattle,
over all the earth and over every creeping thing that creeps
on the earth. So, God created man in His own image; in the
image of God, He created him; male and female He created
them. Genesis1:26-27*

We are unique beings. In all of God's creation on heaven and
on earth there is none quite like us. We have been created in
God's image.

I had an experience one time that brought this point
home to me. During a very difficult period in my life God
pulled back a veil, so to speak, and I was standing before
Him. The Bible says we exist in Him; in fact, everything
exists in Him. This reality is veiled at this time to our
consciousness because God has decided that in this part of
our life, on earth, we walk by faith. But on this day God
pulled back the veil and I was standing before my Father.

It was the most wonderful feeling I have ever
experienced. The amazement at seeing Him took my breath
away. I never could have imagined how comfortable I could

feel with God! I felt like I was home. This is where I came from and this is where I belonged, and I wanted to be with Him forever. I saw this unbelievably wonderful God and I felt like I was a part of Him.

Do you remember the phrase, "He is a chip off the old block" speaking of children who are like their parents? That is what I felt like; I was a teeny tiny chip off this giant block. I never ever, ever wanted to leave Him, it was so wonderful seeing where I came from and also just what I was! I was created in His image, and I came from Him!

My heart was crying out in joy to see Him and be with Him! And you know what? He was enjoying the moment as much as I was. I knew this because we could feel what each other was feeling. We were connected although I was only a tiny speck next to Him. He loved me and I was standing in an ocean of love.

We are created in His image. This is unbelievable and amazing! But what does this mean?

First of all, God is also a tri-part being, so are we. God is a Creator and He has made us also little creators. Oh, but there is so much more. But the point I want to get to is this, like us God feels pain. He loves and His love has made Him vulnerable to pain. He has emotions like we do. Or should I say we have emotions like He does, and this makes us and Him vulnerable. Satan saw this as weakness in God and he thought he could overthrow Him. He saw God's incredible love as weakness.

God's love is not weakness but strength, but He feels pain. This is holy stuff to me. The fact that God feels our pain because He allows Himself to love us, but it goes so much deeper than that. God had a choice to make, a choice that makes Him so vulnerable and causes Him so much pain.

God's Choice

God's choice was whether or not to save us. The Bible tells us, *that God so loved the world that He gave His only begotten Son.* He saved us because He loved us. We all know this but what we don't know is how much He loves us and how much pain and effort it cost Him. All the things that Jesus went through on earth just blow my mind, like His fasting for forty days.

Have you ever tried to fast? I am not good at it. I remember the first time the Lord told me to fast three days, I could not do it. I did not know it at the time, but I was about to face a spiritual battle with the enemy. I just knew the Lord told me to fast for three days. I tried to fast, I made it a couple of meals and then I couldn't stand it any longer and ate and ate. I pulled myself together and tried again. Again, I failed.

As I was sitting there eating my second bowl of peppermint stick ice cream on a chocolate brownie, I commiserated with the Lord over my failure to Him again. I decided I just couldn't do it. This was on a Friday; it was actually Good Friday. The Lord answered me, "Can't you fast for me while I was in hell for you?"

I put down my bowl of ice cream and ran to look at the clock. It was three o'clock. The same time of day Jesus died.

{How does God do this stuff?}

I decided to try again. I fasted from Good Friday at three o'clock until Easter morning. Every time my body screamed for food, I remembered Jesus in hell for me. It wasn't a three-day fast, but I did make it to early Sunday morning, {yes early}, like He asked me too.

I could not fail Him this time knowing of the suffering He went through for me. I made it on a tiny fast and only with God's help but how did Jesus manage for forty days?

I cannot imagine how difficult it was for Jesus too fast for forty days and then be tempted by Satan. But that was nothing compared to what was coming for Him after, the cross.

Jesus' Broken Heart

My daughter Joy shared with me a very special conversation she had with the Lord. Joy was broken hearted. She was a young mother of a one-year old child and she was pregnant again, when she found out her husband was cheating on her with another woman. In fact, she was alone in her bedroom that night knowing he was out with someone else. She was absolutely heart broken and devastated and crushed and felt she had nothing left to give her children, and she asked the Lord, how could she go on?

The Lord told her, "When I was in hell for three days for you, every piece of my heart was totally shattered into pieces. But every piece of my broken heart still loved you. Even in brokenness you can love."

I wept when Joy told me this. God's love for us is just so great. In fact, I can't help but cry when I write this. In her most desperate hour, this gave her strength to go on and care for her children. God chose this for Himself. He allowed Himself to be crushed for us. He experienced a broken heart. His great love for us caused Him to allow Himself to be broken and crushed for us. It made Him vulnerable. Satan pounced on that vulnerability and worked his destruction on Jesus, body, soul and spirit.

I don't know why, but the time that Jesus spent in hell fascinates me. I can hardly wrap my mind around it. How did Jesus endure and overcome? I have always wanted to know more. I recently learned more, from a book I read called *Heavenly Visitation,* by Kevin Zadai.

Kevin died during surgery and during that time he saw Jesus and Jesus taught him some important things. Also, Jesus mentions to Kevin His time in hell.

I have to tell you something, this thrilled me to no end. It was like finding treasure. I had only borrowed the book, but I will buy a copy and read it and read it over and over again, so I can grasp it. I will briefly sum up what thrilled me so much.

Jesus explained to Kevin how Satan operated in hell. He throws our failures in our faces and torments us with them. He reminds us of our losses, our weaknesses and where we have gone wrong. He removes hope and replaces it with eternal torment.

{Has this ever happened to you? It has me and it is pure torment! My failures are pure pain to think about, and I have a lot of them. Now I know where those thoughts come from!}

Satan tormented Jesus for His seemingly failed mission to bring God's kingdom to earth. He mocked Him that He was not the Son of God, and he belittled Him for not taking him up on his offer to bow and worship him when he tempted Him in the wilderness.

How did Jesus endure? One of the ways was He had scripture memorized and He held onto the truth of the word. And I want to quote a small passage from the book.

He was extremely passionate when He talked about his anguish of separation from God. He said He had to go deep within Himself to rehearse and

remember His identity with the Father because circumstances were screaming the opposite.

{So that's what I need to start doing!!!!!}

Jesus overcame not for Himself but for us. He is not the One beating us over the head with our failures! He is the One who has overcome our failures for us! Even though He never failed He does know how it feels to be faced with failure. He went through it.

For we do not have a High Priest who cannot sympathize with our weaknesses, but was in all points tempted as we are, yet without sin. Hebrews 4:15

We truly serve a God who is like us, He feels and hurts like we do, and He knows all about pain. He chose to suffer for us and with us. We are created in the image of God, yes, but Jesus went further than that, He laid aside His deity and became like us in every way. He knows how it feels to have a broken heart.

Chapter Three

Satan: The Soul Shatterer

Be sober, be vigilant; because your adversary the devil walks about like a roaring lion, seeking whom he may devour.
1 Peter5:8

Satan's goal for us is total destruction. He is behind every evil unleashed on mankind. He is behind every sickness, disease, every perversion, wars, torture and every trap that can waylay the human soul. His ultimate goal is to shatter our hearts into a million pieces.

He wants to begin early, in the womb. The devil frequently targets the child in the womb. All three times that I was pregnant were the three hardest times in my life. Satan's plan is to bring havoc to children while they are still in the womb, and he even tries to convince the mother to destroy the child through abortion. Satan wants to create trauma in children's lives so he can begin to take their souls captive.

This was true with me also. My twin sister and I were born under difficult circumstances. We were born to a single teen-age mother who was put out by her parents and had nowhere to go.

It was the worst time of my mother's life. My mother intended to marry our father and even had a wedding shower, she headed off happily with him to his hometown only to find out he already had a wife and three children. My mother had nowhere to go. She stayed in a camper in his yard until just before we were born when her brother and his wife took us in.

I did not know this until my mid-thirties. It helped me to understand myself; I had always felt like I did not belong in this world. I could never shake that feeling. I felt I had no right to be here, or anywhere.

Mom had always told my sister, Carol and I, that we had a fight in her womb before we were born. We had always assumed I won because I was born first, which didn't make sense to me because Carol was always the stronger of the two of us. She was smarter, got better grades and even now she is much healthier than I am.

The Lord showed me I lost the fight; we were struggling not to be born. I was born rejecting my life. I would relive this in a small way every morning when I would wake up. I did not want to wake up, I did not want to face the day. I was still rejecting my life.

Suddenly this made sense to me also, my reaction to stress and fear is to curl up in a ball in the closet, in the dark and cry and beg God to take me, I frequently felt like I did not like life. I was trying to get back into the womb, a place that felt safe.

Many others also suffer things they don't understand, like I did. The devil tries to traumatize children even from the womb. And just because we do not remember the trauma does not mean it does not still affect us, it does because Satan keeps that part of us in torment.

Fragmented Souls

In Anna Mendez Ferrell's book called *Regions of Captivity;* Anna teaches how Satan uses trauma, deep fear and emotional pain to fragment our souls. When Satan manages to get a fragment of our souls, he takes it captive and imprisons it in regions of darkness and torments us. Our souls are made up in such a way that each fragment looks like another one of us.

I was so glad to read her book because I had been to this region in prayer, but I did not understand what I was seeing. I have seen, in my prayers, family members imprisoned, in cave like jail cells, wrapped in chains and tormented and guarded by demons. I have broken out captives from these places through prayer. Her book gave me so much more understanding on what I was seeing. One person can have many pieces of their soul held captive in many different areas. Depending on which part of your soul the devil has captive, the devil has control over the person in that area, and the person that is captive cannot get victory.

Anna gave many examples in her book. As a child Anna's brothers and sisters put a large moth down the back of her blouse. She screamed in terror trying to get it out, but they just laughed at her. This caused her a deep fear of butterflies and moths. Even as an adult she would lose her composure at the sight of a moth, and she could not seem to get rid of her phobia. Anna found part of her soul imprisoned in a dark cell tormented by large black moths. Once she freed her soul from this prison she was no longer tormented at the sight of a butterfly or moth.

This is just a small example of how Satan shatters a

soul and torments it. There are many examples and reasons this happens. Some are reliving torments such as being raped or abused. Some are being held back from serving the Lord, some are kept in poverty.

When someone's soul is being held captive, they will not be able to get the victory in the area they are imprisoned in.

A Fear of Animals

When I was very small my mother had a brief marriage to a very abusive man. He did so much damage to my sister and I that we still are struggling in areas even with all the healing we have had already. I remember the sexual abuse, my sister does not, but she shared a memory with me not too long ago that helped me realize why I have always been so afraid of animals. I have never been able to pet a dog or cat. I used to be so terrified of animals that I couldn't stand to be around them, but my husband has brought home so many animals I got used to that part, but still, I could not touch them. I can't stand to feel an animal, but worse yet if I see a mouse, I absolutely go ballistic. It just didn't make sense to me.

I decided one day I was going to pet my husband's dog, Sam. I gathered all my composure and sat down and petted him. I heard my kids cry out in shock, "Look mom is petting the dog!" I thought maybe that would cure me, but it didn't, I could do it only if I took all my concentration and made myself.

Well, Carol and I discussed her memories not too long ago, and she remembers someone holding up dead mouse in front of us and forcing us to put it in our mouth. When she told me about it, I knew it was true, I even knew where it happened, in a workroom in the basement. Even years after our stepfather had gone Carol and I could not go in that room.

Even though I can't remember this incident, I still feel torment me every time I see an animal, or one touches me. This how Satan operates, he fragments our soul through trauma and keeps that part of us in torment. This is why when we are praying, we are finding pieces of our souls in guarded caves reliving the torment. And every time I see a mouse, or an animal touches me that part of my soul responds.

Anna Mendez describes in her book how some people are imprisoned from birth in parts of their soul. They are imprisoned there from past curses from ancestors. Her book is fascinating, and I highly recommend it. It describes how and why Satan tries to shatter us in pieces.

The Soul Has Many Layers

I heard another Christian teacher on the soul, named Kat Kerr. She explained more about the soul. She described how our souls have layers and each layer of the soul looks just like us. She described our soul as a book with many pages and each page looks like a carbon copy of us. In her ministry she prays for pieces of our souls which have been deposited into other people through illicit sex. As she prays and she sees people's souls being released she describes seeing images of people coming out of them and copies of people returning to themselves.

So illicit sex is another way our soul becomes shattered and left deposited in sex partners. God created us to only be joined in marriage, "And the two shall become one flesh." What is damaging through illicit sex can be healing within the bounds of marriage. Just as each cell of our bodies carries the DNA of our being so do the pieces of our shattered hearts. Satan in his hatred and jealousy shatters us and imprisons us, this is his goal.

Weapons of Mass Destruction

Just as there are many weapons on earth inspired by Satan there are many weapons in the spirit realm that are used against us. I have frequently seen swords and knives in people I have been praying for. I have also seen barbs and vices and chains wrapped around people. In times on earth when torture was used, we see the utter cruelty of Satan. He is behind these weapons both in the physical realm and in the spiritual realm.

In the Middle Ages the tortures were especially heinous and barbaric. There were all kinds of hideous devices that tortured individuals. These tortures were so barbaric it is hard to believe human beings could carry out such evil on each other. There were beds of nails, head crushers; sharp implements that were inserted in private places and wheels that would crush bones.

These hellish devices are inspired by Satan, and he also uses these things in the spirit realm. One of Satan's goals has been to literally bring hell to earth. We have seen this happen during especially evil eras such as the tortures of the Middle Ages or Hitler's gas chambers and ovens that murdered the masses during World War 2. There is no depth to Satan's cruelty.

There are those in this world that can't function because the devil has some part of their souls or even many parts of their souls held in prisons in constant torment.

Satan's goal for you is destruction. He wants to

destroy you because he is in violent opposition to God and everything good, and you are created in the image of God.

Can you imagine Satan's delight when he got his hands on Jesus? He used all his torments and tortures on Jesus. He literally ripped Him to shreds. Why did God allow Satan to torment Jesus? Why does God allow abuse to happen to us?

Chapter Four

Suffering Abuse

But you have seen, for You observe trouble and grief, To repay it by your hand. The helpless commits himself to You; You are the helper of the fatherless Psalms 10:14

Both my husband and I were very broken people seemingly from birth. But it affected us both differently. Jim was born being rejected and not wanted and it caused him to rebel causing a split personality in him. So, he had multiple personalities while I was born in fear and never developed any personality at all. We were total opposites.

Jim's mother was in a very bad marriage, and she had four babies almost four years in a row. First two girls, then two boys, Jim being the second boy and then Jim's mother remarried and had another boy. So, Jim was the fourth child and the middle boy. Jim was the lost child in his family.

Jim's mother dealt with him by keeping him locked in the closet. Jim had told me about this but not in much detail because he rarely ever talks about his past. So, I just assumed this was only for a period while he was small. I later found out this wasn't so.

I also knew Jim ran away when he was fourteen years old. He managed to get from Detroit to Tennessee. There he was apprehended by authorities and put in a juvenile hall. He was there for a while because he refused to tell them who he was. Eventually they found out who he was and put him on a bus back to Detroit. I asked him one time what happened when he got home; hoping his desperate cry for love was noticed. Jim told me his mother locked him back in the closet. I was dumbfounded; he was still being locked in a closet at age fourteen!

Besides suffering from rejection Jim also suffered from verbal, physical and sexual abuse. He never knew what normal was. Several times he almost died, once when he was stabbed, another time when he was hit by a car, another time he was wounded by a gun. Jim's soul was severely damaged. He developed alternate personalities that were not his own.

They were demonic personalities that stunted his real personality, and they grew up in its place. Jim walked around in utter confusion. He lumped all the abuse together in one big mass and blamed society, believing that everyone was unified together to destroy him, and he was at war with the world.

Obviously, Jim wasn't able to function normally. He was trouble. He lashed out at society with rage, fighting and stealing. He began being incarcerated young, in his early teens, frequently being locked up in juvenile hall, the house of correction, county jails and eventually prison.

His broken heart was searching for love but not finding any and it left him vulnerable to those who prey on such young people. One such was a mafia kingpin, who taught him to drive and helped him get a driver license but only so he could steal cars for his chop shops. I didn't even think or realize what it would be like for a young person with no nurturing whatsoever. I did not have that problem. My dad taught me to drive when I was twelve. He let me practice on back farm roads. I got a driver's license the day I turned sixteen.

One time when Jim and I had been married only about five years and we had two toddlers; Jim brought home a young man. We lived in a small town, on the main street in a dumpy apartment over an insurance company, in an ancient old building. Jim was coming home late one night, and he saw a young man sleeping in a cardboard box in a store entrance way, trying to get out of the wind. Jim woke him up and brought him home. He stayed off and on and we did not know his age or where his parents were.

One day he stole our car and went on a joy ride tearing up the exhaust system. We had to junk the car and I was angry at first. But through this we found out he was twenty years old, and his parents had nothing to do with him. He had elderly grandparents that let him stay if he needed to but weren't helping him grow up.

Suddenly it made sense to me. Of course, he would steal our car, he was old enough to drive but he had no way to learn to drive or get a driver's license. He was only fulfilling a natural longing to drive a car. I wondered if there were a lot of young men stealing cars for the same reason.

This was also Jim; he was left to learn from all the wrong teachers about every area of life. Love, sex, money, every area of life which he had a natural need to know about was guided by evil men and women, fulfilling their own wicked desires.

Broken hearts leave us vulnerable. Those who have never known love often become victims to those who prey on their need to love. Pimps hang out in bus stations to find run-aways. They can easily spot young girls or boys who have fled awful home lives. The pimps offer them friendship but only to make sex slaves out of them.

Sexual deviants do the same thing. They prey on young people who need the love of a parent but turn the relationship into a sexual one confusing the broken-hearted young person.

Jim's whole life went from one confusing situation to another, even after he became a Christian at age nineteen. The abuse Jim suffered caused Jim to be a broken person. He had multiple personalities warring within him, and he seemed to have no control of them. He could not function normally; he had no idea what love even was. {God told me that.} He was at war with the world, and he seemed destined to live his life incarcerated.

I was broken also; me and my twin sister, Carol, we also could not function. Where Jim was aggressive, I was the opposite. I cowered in fear. My nightmare was over when I was seven years old, and my mother married my new dad. He adopted Carol and me a year later. The abuse stopped.

The problem was that even though our storms had passed, no one seemed to know we hadn't survived the storm; in fact, no one seemed to even know we had been through a storm. I was dead inside, but I was expected to live. No one understood that we were suffering. They expected something of us we were not able to give them, we did not even know how. I had absolutely no relationship with myself. I could not reason things out, because I had no inner conversation, I was empty. I never thought things through or had any comprehension of things, I was just a blank slate.

It is hard to describe but I will give you an example. In fourth grade I sat next to a popular girl who made fun of an overweight boy that got off at my bus stop. I would laugh with her because that was what I was supposed to do. Then when I got off at the bus stop, he would beat me up. I did not know why. That was how blank I was. I had no inner reasoning.

Our parents would at times become furious with us. I remember one Easter; Carol and I went to the breakfast table and there was a clear plastic Easter egg on the table with a note inside. It was the beginning of a scavenger hunt our parents had prepared for us. Maybe normal kids would have picked up the egg and opened it or asked. "Is this for me?"

But Carol and I could not do that. The egg on the table presented a dilemma. We did not know how to respond. We dare not hope it was for us, we dare not say anything. We never felt that comfortable anywhere or that we had a right to anything. We looked at each other nervously wondering what to do.

Were they going to give it to us?

What should we do?

We ate breakfast silently, frozen by the presence of the egg.

Our parents became enraged that we did not pick up the egg and yelled at us. We recoiled in tears, feeling fear and confusion terrified by our parent's anger. I never seemed to know what would set my parents off, although they seemed to think we should know better, but to us it was like we were walking on a mine field continually, not just at home but also at school. An explosion could happen at any time, a situation that caused us more pain and more confusion. Life was something to be endured.

No one understood our inner suffering. No one ever even acknowledged it was there. We certainly could not have explained it to anyone.

Carol and I had each other. We had our own world. We played with our dolls constantly. Whereas we could not express ourselves whatsoever, our dolls could say and do anything. Even in high school we came home and played with our dolls, we played with them every day and slept with them every night.

There are so many people who are walking around broken from abuse. They look normal on the outside, but they are shattered in a million pieces on the inside. They face misunderstanding, criticism and anger from others because they don't respond like a normal human being, they are broken, and this only adds to their pain.

They may turn to sex, longing for some kind of love. They may turn to drugs and alcohol longing for some kind of relief for their pain. They don't have the ability to make decisions based on reason, but they are led by a huge inner need. They may marry the wrong person, never plan for their future or just exist from day to day, just surviving, not really living.

Jim and I both put our lives in the hands of the Lord. Jim when he was nineteen, I, when I was fourteen. He alone understood our pain, our brokenness, and our needs.

That did not mean that the church understood us, especially Jim. He was supposed to repent and then never sin again. That was more than he could handle. His underdeveloped personality was overshadowed by two demonic ones. He was rarely in control but continuously plagued by guilt and shame.

I didn't have Jim's problem because I was so afraid of other people, I became overly compliant, and a complete goody two shoes to avoid any kind of confrontation which would increase my constant fear, my fear of people, of life

33

and especially of disapproval. So, I looked good on the outside, but was a complete mess on the inside.

I can't describe how intense emotional pain is. I have gone through a lot of physical pain. I have had surgery ten times, cancer and I have had kidney stones three times, gall stones, hernias, irritable bowel, migraines, etc. I know about pain.

I have never had any interest in studying books on physical healing; I did not care about physical healing. That pain is bearable. I have devoured books on inner healing for over thirty years. I want out of emotional pain!!!!!

There are millions of people walking around with broken hearts. They have suffered abuse. They may look fine on the outside, but their hearts have been shattered into a million pieces. They have to limp around emotionally trying to function while no one even acknowledges their pain.

Is there an answer?
Is there hope?
Does God even care
Yes
Yes.
Yes!

Chapter Five

Falling Through the Cracks

See I have inscribed you on the palms of My hands;
Your walls are continually before Me. Isaiah 49:16

There are many of us who fall through the cracks of life, and I am including myself. Life doesn't work for us. We see others around us living normally, and we wonder "Why not me?" It is like we are standing outside looking in the windows at others gathered around a warm fire while we are standing in the cold.

It hurts.

My friend Paul who I wrote about in the foreword fell through the cracks of life. My husband Jim fell through the cracks, growing up in the closet, in the dark. While he heard his brothers and sisters in the house, and he wondered why his mother did not love him.

I know how it feels also to be out in the cold. When I

was little and had no father and my mother worked. I wanted to be home with a mother and father who loved me, instead I was always with some babysitter who usually could barely tolerate me, again, on the outside looking in.

Or some of us fall through the cracks through divorce. I know how that feels too. Dad has a new wife, mom has a new family and suddenly my family is nowhere, never to be seen again. Now my parents have other families and again I am left out in the cold. I really don't know how little children survive this. I was almost twenty when it happened to me and the pain was so great, I didn't think I would survive. How do little kids go through this? Is it any wonder so many young people commit suicide?

Or how about as adults, we can't seem to make it. I used to feel out in the cold again on Sunday's, knowing all the others at church were going home to a Sunday dinner while I was taking my children home to an empty fridge. Or the years I spent driving through neighborhoods longing for a house of my own. Other people had them, why not me?

People fall through the cracks in many ways. The girl whose mother remarries, and her new stepfather molests her, or even, God forbid her real father. She goes on each day as if nothing were happening, just wishing she could go to bed and sleep at night.

Or some people fall through the cracks because of health reasons. Their failing health robs them of a normal life.

There are many ways to fall through the cracks, poverty, prison, mental illness. Or how about those of us that work every day and we just can't make enough money to make ends meet or worse yet lose a job?

Some of us may live our whole lives broken, in a jail cell, or a hospital or even in a cardboard box on the street or a tent in the woods or in a car.

Some of us are born in the crack of life and can't ever seem to get out.

Is there any hope for those of us who fall through the cracks?

Are we destined to just always be on the outside looking in and wondering why life doesn't work for us?

There is Hope

The answer is yes. YES! YES! YES! There is hope!

In fact, I want you to take off your shoes because you are standing on holy ground!

You are closer to God than anyone on earth! You are on God's priority list! Of all the people on this earth, God is most concerned about you!

God's Priority List

My sister Carol discovered God's priority list while praying for my husband Jim. My husband Jim has struggled with his own salvation his whole life. He does not feel good enough to be saved or loved. He often wonders if he will make it to heaven and he is afraid to die.

One day Carol was praying for Jim. She felt she had the perfect solution. She told the Lord, "You should take Jim to heaven for a visit. Then Jim could see for himself that You love him."

Carol was surprised to hear the Lord almost audibly. In fact, they actually had a conversation talking back and forth. The Lord replied, "Because if I brought Jim to heaven he would not want to return, and I would not make him. But I haven't ruled that out."

When Carol told me this it touched me deeply. First

because the Lord had actually thought of that and secondly because the Lord is so loving He would not force Jim to come back if He did. {I just love the Lord!]

Carol and Jesus continued to converse and finally Carol asked Him, "Lord, why are you talking to me like this, You usually talk in an impression, or through scripture?"

He answered, "Because you are praying for Jim, and he is on my priority list. He is like the one sheep I left ninety-nine to find."

Priority list! God has a priority list!

You just don't know how this thrills me!

Are you seeing the hope now!

If you have fallen through the cracks of this life, you go to the top of God's list. Did not Jesus tell us that He would leave the ninety-nine sheep to search out the one sheep who is lost?! Then He will pick you up and carry you!

The Bible tells us over and over again that God is close to the broken hearted. He is so close He takes on our pain and joins us. In fact, to help those who are broken has become the same as helping Him.

If you are in a prison cell, God is there! God's grace rests on prisons in greater measure. If you are living in a box, God is there! If you are brokenhearted, downtrodden, alone or depressed, God is there.

God has listed those throughout the Bible who are special to Him.

They are

The brokenhearted

The hungry and thirsty

The widow

The orphan

The poor

Those in prison

Those who are sick
Those who are weak
Those trapped in sin

We saw this in Jesus ministry. The people others hated, He made a priority. If you have fallen through the cracks of life and you seem to be worthless to the world, I want you to rejoice! You are on the top of His list. You have become His priority. There is hope for you! There is great hope!

God is reaching out to you in love. He understands your pain and you are His top priority. You are by no means lesser than anyone else and especially not to God.

If we were to look at the life of Jesus, we could say that He fell through the cracks of life? He wandered around, never married, He made a lot of important people mad, and they killed Him. To the people of His time, He looked like a failure, because they did not see the whole picture. They thought Jesus was going to be an earthly king. They thought He failed His mission. They judged Him by earthly standards; He did not look very successful.

But He did not fail His mission, He completed His mission in an eternal victory that overcame evil forever, not just for a generation.

If you pass through this lifetime without making a lot of money, you are not a failure. Actually, Jesus never made a lot of money.

If you pass through this world without buying a house or a car or anything of importance you are not a failure. Or if you pass through this world without making any kind of a name for yourself, that will not make you a failure.

If you are alone, you are not a failure.

If you are sick, you are not a failure.

If you have made huge mistakes, you are not out of the game.

But you cannot pass through this life without Jesus.

And if in your life, you call on God and you move toward God, no matter how broken or down and out you may be, you have just become successful.

Chapter Six

Hope

Through whom we also have access by faith into this grace in which we stand and rejoice in hope of the glory of God. And not only that, but we also glory in tribulations, knowing that tribulations produce perseverance and perseverance character and character, hope. Now hope does not disappoint because of the love of God has been poured out in our hearts by the Holy Spirit who was given to us. Romans 5:2-5

I used to not think much of hope. Hope did not change anything, I needed faith. And so many times my hopes were crushed. I have since changed my mind. We have to have hope to keep going. I needed hope because I based my whole life on a couple of things that I felt that God had promised me. And hope was the fuel for my faith. God had to keep me in hope.

Soon after I married, I realized I was in way over my head. Jim was way out of control. He drank and used drugs. I hardly ever saw his true personality anymore and he was constantly manifesting demonic personalities which were awful. He got in fights, had terrible mood swings which could start at the drop of a hat and could scream and break things for hours. He broke every rule in every book, including stealing and was constantly in trouble.

It was like trying to live your life with earthquakes going on. Everything is fine for a while and then an earthquake, and another and another, and then things might be peaceful for a while, but I always knew another earthquake was going to upset my world soon. But my earthquakes were invisible to the rest of the world, and I felt alone with no one earth to go to for help, except God.

Every time I turned to God, He offered me hope and comfort. God started giving me promises. He promised if I were obedient to Him that there was hope for my future. Then He promised me that Jim would not go to prison anymore.

God was committed to me to keeping my hopes up. I believed God, most of the time but there were a couple of times that I thought that things had gotten so bad that even God could not fix them and fell into total despair. Both those times God spoke to me audibly letting me know He was still in control, and as long as I knew He was still in control I could go on. He was always there; He was always faithful to His promises.

My whole life, my reaction to trouble is to want to curl up and die, but God had to keep me moving in faith and in my life. I had to, it wasn't just me and Jim anymore, I had three children to think about. I could not hide in the closet and cry for hours anymore, I had to keep going.

I had to learn how to keep going after a terrible upset. The first thing I learned to do in trouble was to turn to God. Then I would calm down my kids. Sometimes I would keep them home from school, because I would not expect them to function like nothing happened.

I don't like television watching I think it is a waste of

time, but it was one of the best ways I could calm down my emotionally upset children after another of our earthquakes. I invested in the Hanna Barbara videos of the Bible. That was a stretch for my budget, and I chose between those and a washing machine, but the videos were more important to me. My kids watched them over and over.

The next thing was to do the next thing. I would look around and see what needed to be done. I no longer allowed myself to retreat. Usually, for me, with a family of five I always had a sink and counter full of dirty dishes. With shaking hands and shaky knees, I would wash the dishes.

Something happened to me through the years; I stopped hating to do dishes. Washing dishes has become a comfort to me. I made myself do it to keep moving and now I actually enjoy washing dishes. It's my favorite chore. But it started because it was my way to keep functioning when my world was falling apart.

God has offered me hope sometimes on a daily basis. When my husband Jim would be in a seemingly hopeless state and it seemed like the end again, God has come through again and again.

One time things seemed hopeless and Jim and I got in the car and drove to a Christian function in a near-by town. It was all we could do to get there because of the tension we were going through.

Jim was not used to being responsible for anyone including himself and the pressures of trying to support a family with no education, {ninth grade] and facing a world that he felt was against him he was ready to go back to the world he knew before. {I guess that would be stealing and jail.}

As we pulled into the auditorium I wondered if the Lord would do a miracle again. What could happen in this meeting that could fix things for us?

The first thing that happened was once we got inside, and the singing started, I realized in the turmoil I hadn't eaten, and I started to get sick. I suffered from low blood sugar. Immediately I thought we would have to leave, but as I worshipped my blood sugar rose and I felt better. I knew God was in control.

Then the speaker got up to speak. I was amazed. The speaker had also been in the mafia, like Jim and had become a Christian. His story was fascinating, and Jim was on the edge of his seat. Also, like Jim the man had testified honestly against his boss after becoming a Christian. The twist in this man's story was after having been promised a deal for his testimony when he stood before the judge, the judge declared, "I don't care what you have been promised I am the judge, and you are going to prison."

This man survived against all odds having multiple contracts on his life. Jim could relate to this man all the way. Jim also spent time in "the hole", solitary confinement, while in prison because the warden received word of a contract on his life, which I suspect was from the mafia also.

I sat in awe of God, and I wondered as I always do, "How do you do this stuff God? How do you always seem to move heaven and earth just for us?"

Even though the crowd was huge, and we were at the back of a large auditorium Jim was determined to talk to the speaker. Again, God provided, Jim ran to the podium as soon as the service ended. And again, the man was standing there as if waiting for Jim. Jim approached him and the man talked to him as someone who knew just what he was going through. He encouraged Jim and prayed for Jim and Jim left encouraged. His hope once again was restored.

This was only one time God came through with hope

when Jim or I needed it. I have seen this happen again over and over. One time Jim was so distraught, this was on a Sunday. He didn't even come into the sanctuary at church. He was sitting in the hallway, head in his hands. A very special Christian young man, his name was Gordon, he reminds me of a modern-day Stephen, was up on the podium worshipping and he started to dance, and he hurt his foot. I am sure he wondered why he hurt his foot worshipping the Lord, but it was because he was needed in the hall. When he hurt his foot, he went and sat down in the hall, next to Jim. He spent that whole service next to Jim, ministering to Jim.

But there were so many more times God sent help. A huge big black saint named Brother Glover was driving by and stopped in just when Jim was ready to call it quits again. Another time it was a kind police officer who instead of hauling Jim off to jail, sat him down and talked to him kindly and the next day Jim checked himself into rehab. Over and over God sent Jim hope. These are just a few.

God sent me hope in other ways, but just as often and just as lovingly. I would wonder how God could stay so busy with us and manage to run the rest of the universe.

Hope keeps us going. Hope is the fuel to faith. Hope keeps us looking to God and keeps us moving toward Him one difficult step at a time.

The thing I want you to know is that if you have God, you always have hope. He will move heaven and earth to keep His promises to you. No matter how broken and unable you are to go on, He will sustain you.

God never pushed a button and just fixed my problems, like I wanted Him too. I wanted us to go forward at church at prayer time and leave with all our problems fixed. He did not do that, but He has given me miracle after

45

miracle, some small and some big, as I continue to walk with Him in hope, in trust and faith. And over and over when I have run out of hope, He has renewed it once again.

I have had to walk through my life; it has been like traveling through a long desert. I wanted to press fast forward and just skip to the end, the part where everything is fixed, but that has not happened. But what has happened is no matter what I have been through, God has been there, He has kept His promises and He keeps giving me hope, one step at a time.

Chapter Seven

God's Grace

"All that the Father gives Me will come to me and, and the one who comes to Me I will by no means cast out." John 6:37

God does not pick and choose through those who come to Him. He does not reject someone because they are just too evil. It always surprises me when someone thinks that they are too bad, that God is angry with them and does not want them. No matter how bad or broken someone may be, God still wants them.

God's grace is just so incredible. It took me many years being married to Jim before I finally started to get it, many years! There is the idea floating around the body of Christ that once we get saved from that point on, we have to be good. I also believed this and tried my best to be a goody two shoes.{At least on the outside, my insides were still a mess}

This is a very good point and Jesus was always telling people to go and sin no more but where does that leave people like my husband Jim? {Or the rest of us} He had only known chaos his entire life and that was his normal. He was too broken to be able to control himself, he seemed much of the time to be totally out of control.

Jim came to the Lord when he was nineteen years old. He was an absolute mess! As I said, at the time he was a protégé of a mafia boss who was the only male who showed in any interest in Jim, in his life. And even though he was a very wicked man he did do Jim some good. He taught Jim to drive, and he taught him the trade of a cook and had Jim working in his restaurants.

Jim was not able to go and sin no more! He had never had a normal relationship in his life! His soul was very damaged, and he was controlled by two separate demonic personalities that warred within him. He had been committing felonies since he was an early teen and had spent many years locked up.

The court system sent Jim to a psychiatrist to have Jim evaluated and the psychiatrist declared that Jim was "trouble looking for a place to happen," and he was correct. In fact, Jim committed the crime he spent time for in prison after he was saved, he did a string of armed robberies.

Did that mean Jim was no longer saved? Did God give up on Jim? Was Jim just too bad, too messed up or not save able?

No, no, no and no, because of God's grace!

[One thing I do want to point out though is this; Jim has always tried to live a Christian life. The most important thing to Jim is God. Jim has been a soul winner since he got saved, he loves to tell others about the Lord. But still Jim's life was a mess.]

Jim was not too bad for God. In fact, God has told me over and over through the years that He is very pleased with Jim and Jim has a higher place in heaven than I do. God had a plan for Jim's life!

God's immediate plan for Jim was prison. Jim was a criminal and he needed to be locked up. God can't have his children running around the streets with guns holding up businesses. Prison was God's grace to Jim.

If God had not wanted Jim in prison, he certainly had the chance to keep Jim out. Jim was not in prison long when he escaped. Jim escaped from a Michigan prison and made it to Colorado where he lived in the mountains for nine months. When he was apprehended, they put him in the county jail in Colorado waiting to be extradited back to Michigan. Michigan had ninety days to retrieve him, or he would have been let go. As the days went by and the Michigan authorities did not arrive Jim began to hope that he would be released. But with just one day to spare they arrived and brought him back to prison.

Jim spent his prison sentence with God's special grace upon him keeping him safe. After Jim was released on parole, he was not able to live on the outside. He violated parole and was returned to prison. I met Jim directly after his second parole and soon after he was locked up again, and then again. Jim had no chance for a normal life, he was just too broken......except for God's grace.

It was at this point Jim, and I got married. I had met Jim when I was seventeen and married Jim when I was nineteen. {Our story is written in my book, *The Impossible Marriage.*}

I remember when I first met Jim. It was right after Jim's second parole. Jim had been reading his Bible and praying. He told me, "God gave me this verse this morning," Jim opened his Bible and read, *"He gives families to the lonely, and releases prisoners from jail, singing with joy!"* {Psalm 68:6 Living Bible]

I often think back to that morning Jim told me that with awe, because that is exactly what God did for Jim. God in His grace and plan for Jim has given Jim a life outside of prison and a family! It was only by God's grace!

Shortly after Jim and I were married I turned to God in prayer realizing that the situation was hopeless, and Jim and I would never make it. God gave me a promise through the verse Isaiah54:9 *"For this is like the waters of Noah to Me; For as I have sworn that the waters of Noah would no longer cover the earth. So, I have sworn that I would not be angry with you nor rebuke you."*

God promised me that Jim would not go to prison again. God had decided to give Jim a life and a family, Jim could not do this on his own, he was too broken. It was only by God's grace. Jim would do good for a while and then commit another felony. Over and over, we have stood before courts facing felony charges, facing prison, facing the end of our life and our family, wondering if maybe Jim had pushed God too far. But over and over God has shown us favor and mercy and grace. Our marriage our life and our family were God's plan, and His grace has kept us, despite of how broken Jim and I were.

This book is written to you, the broken- hearted, the underdog, the lonely and forgotten. I want you to know God has a plan for your life, a good plan. If you cling to Him; He will cling to you. His grace will give you a life, it won't be your plan it will be His plan, but it will be the best plan. But this I can guarantee you, it won't be easy, {nothing worthwhile ever is}.

I really thought all those years ago when God gave me promises about my future that God was going to do all this healing on Jim quickly and then we could have a normal life. Well, that didn't happen, in fact for many years it didn't seem like anything was ever going to get better. But they did, but did I ever get my normal. Well no, not yet, Jim is sixty-six now and he has come a million miles, but he still has a constant struggle. The Lord has shown me Jim won't be completely healed until the day that he stands before the Father, because that is Jim's biggest need, a father. So, I never got my normal; but what is normal?

Chapter Eight

What is Normal?

These things I have spoken to you, that in Me you may have peace. In the world you will have tribulation; but be of good cheer I have overcome the world. John 16:33

I have always felt like Jim and I and our family were broken and everyone else was normal. I longed for us to be normal. All I wanted was normal!

To me normal was having a husband that was not an alcoholic and did not get drunk and scream all night. Normal was not having the police at your house and your husband not getting arrested all the time. Normal was having a real home, a car that ran and enough money to pay your bills and cook nice meals. Normal was no fighting and not having holes in all your walls and doors that were smashed up. Normal was having no problems at all!

We all want normal. We don't want our parents to get divorced, that is not normal. We don't want to get cancer, which is not normal. We don't want our spouse to die or leave us or our child to be born handicapped or anything to happen to any of our children. We don't want to lose our job or lose our home or to get in a car accident. We don't want a flood, a hurricane, a tornado or a war, all these things are bad. We do not even want the car to break down or the fridge to break down or actually we don't want any trouble whatsoever. WE WANT NORMAL!!!!

There is no such thing as normal. There are not even any normal people. Everyone has problems, some of us more than others. We have to accept the fact that things are never going to be problem free in this life, life is going to be hard, and things are going to happen that we don't expect. We can't depend on the circumstances around us, they are going to change. Things will happen that we have absolutely no control over. We long for something familiar to hold onto.

Something that Never Changes

Although everything around us may change we have something that will always remain the same, our anchor, our rock, our strong tower, our hiding place. Jesus is our rock. His love will never change, and we can come to rest in His care. He will always be with us; He is always there for us and that will never change. He is our normal. In every situation and in every circumstance, we stay anchored in Him and no matter what the circumstances that are raging around us, we hold firm in Him.

That does not mean that troubles and trials will not come. We may even face death. But His care transcends life and death, physical and spiritual or anything that can come against us.

I think of the insanities of World War 2. It was horrible beyond words. The Jewish people and many others faced unbelievable atrocities. Their children were shot down with machine guns while the parents were herded up like cattle and brought to death camps. I have seen the pictures of piles of naked dead bodies so thin they look like skeletons, stacked on top of each other and tossed out like garbage. It is hard to believe the horror of it. It was as abnormal as you could get!

The minds of the general public were bent by the perverse and evil Adolph Hitler to believe his hideous lies. Not just the Jews were looked down upon but the elderly the handicapped and also homosexuals, and anyone deemed not perfect.

But there were those whose minds that Hitler could not bend. It was those whose anchor was held fast in God. They do not change with every new wind of popular thinking. They are not moved by evil. They have the unchangeable God within them. He is their normal. Like Him they do not change; they held onto truth.

I think of people during that time like the ten Booms. Casper ten Boom, an elderly watchmaker lived with his two middle aged spinster daughters, Betsy and Corrie. They were quiet people with deep faith in God. When their neighbors the Jews began to be persecuted, they did not follow this new normal. Their hearts were firm. They became part of an underground that hid Jews and moved them to safety.

It began when a Jewish woman entered the watch shop and asked Casper for help. He told her he would always welcome God's people. A false wall was built in their home above the clock shop to hide Jews during a raid. For nearly two years they provided shelter for Jewish people and others who were being hunted by the Nazi's.

Their quiet normal life changed. It became a

nightmare. But anchored in Christ they did not change with it, and they became a hiding place for others. They had put their trust in God alone.

But that does not mean their troubles went away. They didn't. They were caught and sent to a concentration camp, all three of them. There Casper and Betsy died, only Corrie survived. She lived and helped many find healing in the aftermath of the war.

Did God fail Casper and Betsy? No, absolutely not. He never left their side. Corrie described how Betsy died, her face was glowing with peace, and she had a smile on her lips. She whispered to Corrie, "There is no pit to deep that He {God] is not deeper still."

She died holding onto her normal, her normal was love and peace. The hatred of the Nazi's never penetrated her.

So, although our circumstances will never offer us any stability, our normal comes from somewhere else. Our normal is a truth that never falters in the midst of lies. Our normal is a love that never waivers in the midst of hate; our normal is an inner peace that never waivers in the midst of chaos and confusion and our normal is a hope that is never snuffed out in the midst of despair.

Our hope is steady, unchanging and true and it holds through life and through death. Our normal is in God's goodness, His love, His mercy, his faithfulness, righteousness and truth. In Jesus Christ we have an anchor that holds us steady; in Jesus we have normal.

Chapter Nine

Inner Healing Part One

Search me oh God and know my heart; Try me and know my anxieties; And see if there is any wicked way in me And lead me in the way of everlasting. Psalm 139:24

For years I have devoured every book I could find on inner healing. I wanted it!!!! I wanted inner healing. I knew I was a mess and I wanted to be fixed. I stumbled across my first book about inner healing shortly after I had married. The book was so exciting! It was about people that God would heal their memories and they would receive freedom from their troubling pasts.

So of course, I prayed the prayer in the book and waited. I wondered what God would do. I did not have to wait long. That night I woke up and relived a memory. I was surprised because it hadn't happened all that long before. I was about nineteen or twenty at the time and this had happened when I was sixteen. I woke in the middle of the night in terror.

I had forgotten that awful day; I had tucked it away and never thought of it again. I never liked school much except my junior year of high school, because I had a boyfriend and I wanted to see him every day! It was the biggest need in my small little teenage world to be loved by someone, a boyfriend. That need was so strong in me I guess you could say I had a one-track mind, except for Jesus, He held the highest place, and a boyfriend was second.

In Michigan that year we had a huge blizzard, people are still talking about that blizzard, and school was shut down for a whole week. This was not good for a sixteen-year-old girl with a one-track mind. This was devastating to a sixteen-year-old girl with a one-track mind. I could not go to school and see my boyfriend.

After three or four days the roads had opened up enough for my dad to get to work so I decided to ride into town with him to see my boyfriend. I called the boyfriend and told him I was coming and went and got into my dad's car.

My dad was furious.

Now you have to understand something about me and my dad. I loved my dad because his entrance into my life meant the end of abuse, but he scared me. I was not just scared of my dad I was afraid of all men, but my dad was the man I was most afraid of. He was a forceful person.

Even after I was married, and I lived in Florida and dad lived in Michigan I was still scared of my dad. I have always been scared of my dad. My dad was someone you just did not mess with. But I had never seen my dad this mad. I would not purposely ever do anything to rouse his wrath because he terrified me when he was angry. And this was really bad because my mom and sister were not there to hide behind it was just me alone with a very angry man who terrified me.

I did not see this coming. I did not realize I did anything wrong. I was a very self-centered person, and I did not have the ability to see anything other than my own needs. I don't think anyone on earth made my dad as mad as I did because it was like we were both on two different planets.

Dad was angry because he had to drive me, and the roads were bad. He was trying to convey to me how selfish I was, but he was so angry that inwardly part of me died that day. I don't want to say any more than just, it was bad. He did not take me all the way to where I was going, he ejected me from the car and made me walk. So, on shaky legs in utter shock I walked to my boyfriend's house. When I got there, I realized he really did not care if I was there or not.

When I woke up with this memory the pain was as fresh as if it were happening again. I cried for hours, reliving the pain. A little older now I could see my dad's point and I told the Lord, "I was selfish, he was right."

The Lord taught me a lesson I have always remembered. He told me, "You were immature, but you were acting like a sixteen-year-old girl, because that is what you were."

God was giving me permission to have the feelings I did and to be what I was. I did not have to be more mature because I just wasn't there yet.

I had to remember His lesson when I had children of my own. I remember being frustrated with my little boy one day and saying to him, "You're acting like a two-year-old!" Then I realized he was two years old! Of course, he was acting like a two-year-old!

God accepts us at the maturity level we are at. He does not expect more from us than we can give. He is patient with us and our feelings, and even as immature as mine were, they are always precious to Him.

God told me, "You lost the ability to receive correction that day."

This was my first experience with inner healing. It was painful. It meant facing the pain that was buried within me. There was more to come, much more.

I kept reading any book I could find on inner healing, the books fascinated me. One day I put down another book on inner healing and prayed again. I wanted to be fixed! As I prayed the words to a song kept coming through my mind.

"In His time, in His time, He makes all things beautiful in His time." God was telling me to be patient this was going to take time.

God Uses Dreams in Inner Healing

One of the ways the Lord has used for my inner healing is through dreams. He would unveil and uncover things I needed to deal with in my dreams. He was showing me things about myself. He showed me fear had destroyed my personality. {I dreamed of a Christian motel and a horrid vine had grown through it and destroyed all the rooms except one. I was living in a very small room, the only one left. It was very cramped in there. That was my personality destroyed by fear.}

When I wasn't fearful, I was selfish, self-centered and very spoiled. {I did not like that} {I dreamed I was standing up to worship wearing a sequin gown, like I was some kind of movie star.}

My compassion, which is normally a good thing, was out of control and was overcoming my reason.

{I dreamt of a kind lady in our church sitting angrily

on my mother's lap}

When I needed to pay more attention to my children, I dreamed I was staring at an ostrich.

If I was making progress that would show up in my dreams also. In later years when I started to learn to stand up for myself, I dreamed that Mr. T picked me up in a limousine and we kissed.

If you are thinking that you do not know what your dreams mean, I don't know what a lot of my dreams mean either, but if you pray God will show you.

I had one dream, a nightmare, over and over my whole life. I would always wake up shaking in terrible fear. In fact, this dream terrified me so much that I was afraid of dreams because this one nightmare plagued me since I was a child.

I would dream I was looking through a closet and as I pulled back the clothes, I would see a small door. The door would strike terror in my heart because I knew there was something terrible behind it. I would wake up shaking with fear.

After I started to realize God was talking to me through my dreams, I realized this was more than just a nightmare. I realized there was something behind this door I needed to deal with. I decided I would go into my dream in prayer and open that door.

I waited until I had my two little ones down for their nap and I went and sat on the living room couch. I closed my eyes, took a deep breath and went to the back of that closet. I found the little door and I opened it.

Suddenly, I was in another place. I was in my crib, and I was about two years old. I was not looking at myself, I was two again. I was in my crib and standing next to my crib was a man. It was dark and I just saw his form standing there. I was little again and the terror I felt was greater than any terror I have ever felt before.

I could not stand it. I immediately opened my eyes. The terror was too great. I ran and threw myself on the bed where my kids were sleeping and clung to them. I needed someone to hold me!

I knew my stepfather molested me, but I could not face that alone. Later God led me to a counselor and had me make an appointment. As I walked into her office God showed her what happened. I was able to open that door again this time with help. God was there. I went home and told my husband I felt like a different person. I knew what was lurking in the shadows now. I never had that nightmare again.

God was restoring the person in me, but it didn't happen overnight. I already mentioned in this book how God brought me back to my birth also. He had me ask my mother about my birth and then I literally remembered being born and rejecting my life. That was another big step. I was thirty-three by that time.

I really believed until that time I had no right to be here.

God told me, "This is my earth, I put you here and you have a right to be here."

Another big step in my inner healing came at a prayer meeting. I was a prayer hog. I could never get enough. It gave me relief from my turmoil.

This night I was at a lady's prayer meeting at church, and they always had a chair in the middle for anyone who wanted prayer could sit in. As the ladies prayed for me the leader said, "Summer, I see that you have problems and you get prayer, but it is only on the surface. It is never really the real issue because the real you is encased in a hard shell. It is like the outer surface of this shell gets dealt with, but nothing can get under to the real issues the real you is under a shell."

I had never heard of such a thing. I wasn't sure what she was talking about. They continued to pray until they saw a crack in the shell appeared. All I knew was when they saw the crack appear, I felt pain and started crying.

Maybe I did have a personality after all; maybe there was a person inside of Summer! Only God knew and only God could fix her!

God knows what is wrong with us and He knows how to fix us. That is what He is going to do. We don't have to beg Him it is His plan. We do have to cooperate with Him though. We need to want to get better and to follow His leading. And that is not easy, it is hard, very hard.

Chapter Ten

Inner Healing Part 2

My brethren, count it all joy when you fall into various trials, knowing that the testing of your faith produces patience. But let patience have its perfect work, that you may be perfect and complete lacking nothing. James1:4-5

There is more to inner healing than prayer. There is work, lots and lots of hard work. One of the early things God started dealing with in my life was the ability to take rejection. I could not handle rejection at all. It was severe. If anyone just disagreed with me, I would start feeling the room spin. I could not handle real life because I might have to face rejection. I hid at home with the kids and let Jim face life. He was not afraid of people.

I could not even handle a telephone solicitor. They would call to sell me something and I would tell them I had no money, but they would not leave me alone. I dreaded the phone. They would call Jim and he would just slam the phone down. I was in awe. I did not have the courage to do that. {Now, I do.]

When God started to deal with my ability to receive rejection, He did not tell me what was coming but I started to get rejection everywhere I went. I thought the world had come to an end. I could not figure out what was happening to me. God taught me to deal with rejection by giving me massive doses of it from many people! He was behind it. He was growing me up. Believe me, it was torture! I didn't get better overnight. I hid in the closet or locked myself in the bathroom crying for years. It was a long hard process.

One of the main lessons I have learned in life is not to take myself out of the situations God puts me in. This is hard, but it is very important. If God puts you in a hard situation to teach you something and you run from it, He will put you there all over again, so you better just face it and learn your lessons.

God has used many different things in my life to grow me up and things like jobs I have had to do, neighbors, pets, my children and especially Jim, fighting for Jim against all odds and the big one, fighting with Jim. I had to learn not to cower in fear anymore, but that took a long, long time.

I found out Jim ruled with an iron fist on our honeymoon. We were in a camper, and he wanted to build a fire one night and sit around the campfire. I did not want to. He said yes and I said no. The next thing I knew he was banging on the side of the camper demanding we build a campfire.

Uh-oh, I've got trouble. Jim told me what I could do and what I couldn't do. If I didn't do it, things got a little rough. My normal manipulation tricks did not work on him either. I was in a heap of trouble. I had to learn to stand up for myself. In the early years of our marriage, I had a few victories, with some smaller issues. I would wait a day or two after Jim had got his way and then I would demand the same thing of Jim that he had demanded of me. But I would hit him with a feather, not a hammer; I would do it with humor.

We would laugh about it and he would say, "I forget

you have a mind of your own." Or sometimes he would say. "Did I really say that to you?"

He was like Ralph Cramden on the honeymooners. He was the king, and I was the nobody. We would watch that show and laugh because it reminded us of us.

One time after we had been married a couple years, Jim decided I was going to buy beer for him. I did the grocery shopping and he told me he was going to put beer on the shopping list, and I was to buy it, he earned the money, he paid for the groceries and if he wanted to drink, he would drink and that was that.

There is nothing in this world I hate more than his drinking! There is nothing in this world I hate more than alcohol! Not to mention Jim was a mean drunk! This was not going to happen.

I have explained in previous books that smelling alcohol on someone's breath is devastating to me. It is like an irrational fear. I literally shake with fear. I need to escape!

World War 3 ensued. Jim was not used to open defiance out of me and we were having a big fight. Suddenly I started laughing and laughing right in the middle of this awful fight. "Jim," I declared, "I can't buy your alcohol, I am not twenty-one!"

It had never dawned on either of us that I wasn't old enough. Oddly enough Jim never asked me again to buy him alcohol, even after I turned twenty-one, and I never did. I poured out tons of it though.

In later years I stood up to him more and more, as I got a little stronger and stronger. Sometimes things even got a little physical.

This may not sound like inner healing to you, but I had to get to a point where I was no longer a cowering victim. I was getting daily practice.

One-time things got a little physical. We had just bought our present house and we were working on getting it ready to move into. We had to move out of our mobile home we had been living in and we had to sell it soon because we could not afford two house payments. We actually did not have any money, at the time, my checkbook was at zero.

As we were working on the house Jim slipped away and got drunk. The problem was as drunk as he was, he would not admit he was drunk and when I took his car keys, he became enraged. I left my car at the new house, and I managed to get him into the back seat of his car to drive back home. He was so angry he started smashing out the car windows. He smashed the front window and then he smashed the back window.

When we got home, he was still in a rage, and I was afraid he was going to begin smashing out the mobile windows. I knew it would spell ruin for us because the mobile home was ready to sell, and we needed it to sell. I managed to knock Jim down and my daughter, and I sat on him.

Jim is extremely strong, but he was drunk enough that he could not get up with the two of us sitting on him and pushing down with all our might. Jim was not hurt but both my knees were black and blue for a week. Finally, he stopped struggling and promised if we let him up, he would go to bed, and sleep and he did.

I told him the next day I wish I had thought of sitting on him twenty years earlier. I never had to do anything like that ever again, because he settled down quite a bit after that. I was glad we had taken his car, so he was the one who had to drive with the smashed windows to remind him of how he acted.

The next day I was not angry with Jim, and he was not angry with me either. We were just both glad the mobile home windows did not get smashed. The reason I had never thought of that earlier was if he got that mad I would run, {I have gone out windows, snuck out the back door anyway I could escape, sometimes with three kids in tow} or I would hide or I would Just sit there frozen in fear with tears running down my face, or begging him to calm down. I did not use to face things.

I have constantly been put in uncomfortable situations, by God. He is answering my desperate prayers for inner healing. These uncomfortable situations stretch me and grow me up, but it does not feel pleasant.

For the past fifteen years I have worked as a home health aide. This job has stretched me to the limit, me, the shy, scaredy cat who wants to run away and not to face people.

The job goes something like this, I receive a name and address from my office of which I have to show up and do something, I was never sure what it would be until I got there. For years each time I received a new client I would walk up to the door with shaky knees, wondering if I would ever be able to do this without fear.

Most of the time everything went fine, but other times it would be like entering a house of horrors. One of my main duties is helping people take showers. Sometimes showing up at a man's apartment, a stranger, then introducing myself and then ten minutes later giving him a shower, well... this is not my idea of fun.

Quitting has not been an option because for the past ten years or so I am the main support of the family. If it hadn't been this way, believe me I would have run and hid!

God has grown me up the hard way. He has grown me up by putting me in hard situations. It is part of inner healing.

Inner healing requires facing your fears over and over and over and you get a little stronger each time. Again, I wanted a quick easy fix, but again it has taken a lifetime or longer of hard work, and I still have a long way to go!

Chapter Eleven

Tender Hearts

And be kind to one another, tenderhearted, forgiving one another, even as God in Christ forgave you. Ephesians 4:32

The condition of our heart is of the utmost importance. God wants our hearts to be tender toward Him. In the Parable of the Sower and the Seed, the soil was the condition of the heart.

"Behold a sower went out to sow. And as he sowed, some seed fell by the wayside; and the birds came and devoured them. Some fell on stony places, where they did not have much earth; and they immediately sprang up because they had no depth of earth. But when the sun was up, they were scorched, and because they had no root they withered away. And some fell among thorns and the thorns sprang up and choked them. But others fell on good ground and yielded a crop: some a hundred-fold, some sixty, some thirty. He who has ears to hear, let them hear!" Matthew 13:3-9

Jesus explains to the disciples that the seed is the word, and the soil is the heart. The heart, which is good ground, bears fruit, a lot of fruit. The stony and shallow hearts don't produce anything. Tender hearts are protected and nurtured by God because they are so precious to Him. It is our hearts that connect with God, not our minds and therefore a tender heart is very important for us and to God.

I learned this when I tried to bug my husband to go to church because he had quit going. This was different; we had always gone to church together. But for a period, Jim stopped going. My motivation for Jim to go to church was because I wanted him to hurry up and get his life together; mainly I wanted him to quit drinking!!!

I hated his drinking so much that even thought of it for one more week was too much. I was always hoping that this would be the week and some miracle would happen at the altar and Jim would quit drinking. {Although some pastors would actually say it was alright to drink alcohol, because Jesus turned water into wine, and that would send Jim into an alcoholic binge for several weeks. Usually, although most times unsuccessfully, Jim was at least trying not to drink.}

So, when Jim stopped going to church, I panicked and began to nag. Finally, God stopped me. He told me, "Stop trying to get Jim to go to church. It is not My will for him to go to church at this time. He will become convicted and try to make changes in his life that he is not strong enough to make and become discouraged. You and the kids go without him."

Jim's tender heart was extremely important to God. In fact, that is one of the reasons that my husband Jim is so pleasing to God although his life had a lot of sin in it. I want to tell you some qualities I have noticed of his tender heart.

Tender hearts are quick to repent. In fact, every time Jim prays, he starts by repenting, and that usually takes a while. Jim always prays at the table and sometimes the food gets cold.

Tender hearts are quick to forgive. Those with tender hearts do not hold grudges, and they usually forgive you whether you ask or not.

Tender hearts are humble. A sure quality of a tender heart is the complete lack of pride. Tender hearts are humble towards God and humble towards others. I have to tell you a little story about this one. When I wrote my first book, *The Impossible Marriage,* I decided if I was going to write our story, I was going to really tell it. So, I did. I asked Jim to read it so if there was something, he did not want in there he could tell me.

That book took me nine months to write. So, for nine months I was preoccupied, I had a pencil and a notebook, and I was writing away. Jim told me later he was happy because I wasn't bugging him to turn the television off. Otherwise, he really didn't think a thing about what I was doing he was just glad I was preoccupied and not bugging him.

I asked Jim, "Don't you want to read what I wrote?"

Jim looked at my pile of scribble and said, "No, I will wait until you type it."

He probably thought that would be the end of it because I never learned to type, and I did not know how to use a computer. Well, after I finished the book, I sat down to type it. For two hours I tried to figure out how to type on the computer that my daughter gave me.

Finally, I got my daughter Joy to come over and show me how. Now I was even busier. I use the one finger typing method and typing that book took all my time. I would get up hours before work and type and then type into the night after work. {If you have read that book, I am sure you have noticed all the mistakes and that after at least fifty times going through and trying to find them. I did not know what I was doing.}

I finally finished and printed up a big stack of papers and delivered them to Jim. Jim took one look and said, "I will read it when you get it published." And he thought that would be the end of it. {He does not enjoy reading like I do.]

Well, the day came when the book was at the publishers and I could not wait to get a copy of it in my hands, I was so excited, imagine a real book!

I asked Jim, "Are you going to read the book when it comes?"

All of a sudden Jim realized I had written a book and he wondered what I wrote in it. He said, "I hope you didn't mention in the book that I have been to prison."

Uh-oh.

I wondered if he was going to kill me.

The book came and Jim put on his reading glasses and buried his nose in the book for a couple of days. After reading it Jim told me, "People are going to hate me."

"Jim," I said, "What you have been through may help someone else."

And that was the end of it. He never even yelled at me. Through the years it was devastating for Jim when he thought someone knew he had been in prison. He always thought people hated him, even though they didn't. I realized what a hard position I put him in, writing it in a book, but the thought of helping someone else made it worth it to him. It amazed me that he never said another word about it. I was starting to see what God sees in him.

Tender hearts are compassionate.

Compassion, of course, is what tender hearts are all about. We feel, we care, we love.

Tender hearts are generous.

A person with a tender heart is not selfish and self-centered. They give to others and sacrifice their own needs.

Tender Hearts are Alert

A heart that is tender is alert to the voice of God. A heart that is tender notices the pain of others. A heart that is tender is alive and feeling.   A heart that is tender can drop everything and change their course.

Many times, hearts become tender through suffering. In my own life I have noticed that I have become tender in an area that I have suffered and do not want anyone else to go through the same thing.

This is a small thing, but it made a huge impression on me. When my sister and I were in sixth grade we got invited to a girl named Debbie's birthday party. It was an overnight party. We rode home with Debbie on the bus because she lived quite a distance from us, way on the far side of town. We actually did not know Debbie that well, but we went anyway and there were several other girls there as well. All of us girls were taken by Debbie's parents to a near-by roller-skating rink.

While we were at the roller-skating rink my sister Carol became very ill. She felt horrible and began vomiting. Immediately we wanted to call our parents and go home. But Debbie's mother did not want her daughter's party spoiled so she just ignored us. We could not use the phone at the roller-skating rink because it was long distance. We had to wait in a cold dingy bathroom, and my sister was very sick while Debbie and her friend's roller skated.

The only one who seemed to care was another girl at the party. Think of it, it was an eleven-year-old girl who sacrificed her fun to help us. She sat in the bathroom with us and helped me tend to my sister. Debbie's mother did not bother.

When we finally got back to Debbie's house, we were able to call my parents and they came and got us, although it took quite a while, because it was snowing, and we were far from home. Still, we got no help from Debbie or her mother; we sat in the bathroom at their house until our parents arrived.

This made an impression on me for life. Even though I was only eleven years old I made up my mind that my pleasure would never be more important than someone who was sick and needed help. I never wanted to do that to another person. I realized that Debbie's mother had a hard heart toward my sister, she had no compassion, and I wanted to be a person with a tender heart. I have remembered that lesson through the years when someone was sick and needed my help.

I have a patient who has suffered terribly with illness. She is so tenderhearted and alert about how other people feel that she notices I don't feel good before I do. She will ask me, "Do you have a backache?"

I had to stop and think about it. I did. "How did you know?" I asked her.

"You kept putting your hand there," she answered.

She frequently notices my aches before I notice them myself. Not mine but others too. While I am working, she will tell me to sit down and rest. She has a tender heart.

We can choose a tender heart. We can choose to not let ourselves become hardened. Tender hearts are always looking outward to others and meeting their needs and not looking to meet selfish desires.

God is cultivating a tender heart in us. This is extremely important. We can choose to cooperate with Him. It is His goal that we become tenderhearted, and our hearts become receptive to Him and His words and then our lives will bear fruit.

Chapter Twelve

Hard Hearts

But in accordance with your hardness and your impenitent heart you are treasuring up for yourself wrath in the day of wrath and revelation of the righteous judgment of God. Romans 2:5

We don't ever want to allow our hearts to get hard. Hard hearts lead to things like judgment and wrath from God. Just as tender hearts are pleasing to God and lead to favor, hard hearts are just the opposite. They lead us away from God, away from life and to our own destruction. We don't want a hard heart!!!!

Hearts can become calloused. They become calloused through pride, through sin, and through rebelliousness. They can also become calloused after much hurt if we don't turn to God, with our pain. Because our inner man, our spirit or our heart is the part of us that has fellowship with God, this condition will cause us to be unable to connect to God.

When Jesus talked about hard hearts it had to do with being able to really hear what He was saying to them.

He said to His disciples, "Why do you reason because you have no bread? Do you not yet perceive nor understand? Is your heart still hardened? Having eyes, do you not see? And having ears do you not hear?" Mark 8:17-18

The condition of our hearts is important when it comes to hearing and seeing with our spiritual senses. Those with a hardened heart are blind and deaf to the spirit realm, the realm in which we contact God.

A Classic Tale

One of my all-time favorite stories is, A Christmas Carol. It is the perfect example of a hard heart. Ebenezer Scrooge had so hardened his heart, that he would not help anyone! He didn't care about the suffering people around him, even though he had the power to help them. Even suffering children didn't move him.

The miracle of the story is that his heart is softened, and he changes. He becomes the total opposite in one night after being visited by three spirits, the ghosts of Christmas past, Christmas present and Christmas future. Scrooge then becomes generous and loving and does good to all around him. I love this story it is a testimony of the beautiful change of a man who chooses to soften his hard heart. Scrooge made that decision.

It is up to us, we can change, like Scrooge did, with God's help. {Yes, I know its fiction}

Hard Hearts Lead to Hell

There is a perfect example of a man who hardened his heart in the Bible; it is the story of the rich man and Lazarus.

"There was a certain rich man who was clothed in purple and fine linen and fared sumptuously every day. But there was a certain beggar named Lazarus, full of sores, who was laid at his gate, desiring to be fed with the crumbs which fell from the rich man's table."   Luke 16:19-20

This is not just a made-up story. When Jesus used the phrase, "a certain rich man" He was telling us a true story, of course, Jesus knows everyone's story. He used this to teach us. This rich man is a perfect example of a hard heart. Every day he passed Lazarus who was starving and sick and he showed no compassion. {A hard heart shows no compassion.}

This rich man did not even give Lazarus his scraps! He simply ignored him. It would not have been any trouble at all for the rich man to have fed Lazarus, but his heart was so hard that he passed by him every day without helping him. The Bible goes on to tell us that both men died. We find out where the rich man's hard heart has led him.

*"And being in torments in hades, he lifted up his eyes and saw Abraham afar off, and Lazarus in his bosom. Then he cried and said, 'Father Abraham, have mercy on me, and send Lazarus that he may dip the tip of his finger in the water and cool my tongue; for I am in torment in this flame.' "*Luke 16:23

The rich man is in hell! This is serious stuff here; we do not want to go where hard hearts will lead us! Warning! Guard yourself against a hard heart!

Divorce and Adultery

I hate divorce and I especially hate adultery. These are signs of a hardened heart. I did not say this, Jesus did.

The Pharisees also came to Him, testing Him, and

saying to Him, "Is it lawful for a man to divorce his wife for just any reason?" And He answered and said to them, "Have you not read that He who made them at the beginning made them male and female, and He said, 'For this reason a man shall leave his father and mother and be joined to his wife, and the two shall become one flesh'?

"So then, they are no longer two, but one flesh. Therefore, what God has joined together, let not man separate."

They said to Him, "Why then did Moses command to give a certificate of divorce, and to put her away?"

*He said to them, "Moses, **because of the hardness of your hearts,** permitted you to divorce your wives, but from the beginning it was not so. And I say to you, whoever divorces his wife, except for sexual immorality and marries another, commits adultery; and whoever marries her who is divorced commits adultery." Matthew 19:3-9*

I want to talk about this because I have seen this over and over. I have seen situations in my life where I cannot believe the hardness of heart that is shown between husbands and wives! One young lady I knew, who was married and had two small children, started talking online to an old boyfriend. She became more interested in him and she hardened her heart to her husband. She began plotting and planning how to leave her husband without it costing her anything. She wanted everything, and she got it, because her husband still loved her and did not put up a fight.

Her cruelty was alarming to me! This was the man she vowed before God to love?! She plotted and schemed to totally destroy him so she could have another man! And she also did this at the expense of her children. Her children were devastated and one of them is still having trouble many years later. This girl was a Christian and saw nothing wrong with what she did. It shocks me to no end how someone can become so hardened to their husband and children and cause them so much pain.

I've seen it again and again. Another couple I knew, the husband left his wife for another woman, with children, knowing he was leaving his wife with no support, and she had nowhere to live, and knowing this woman's children would have no mother. This man was a pastor! And all the while claiming he was right with God! The hardness of his heart toward his own wife shocked me. He did not care a thing for her, he had hardened his heart.

People who commit adultery have to harden their hearts to continue their sin. One friend of mine, whose husband was cheating on her, he would always pick a fight so he could have an excuse to leave the house and go see another woman. Well, she figured out what he was up to, and she stopped falling for his fights. She remained sweet and didn't take the bait. When fighting with her did not work he began to pick on his own son! She was whipped she couldn't allow her son to be picked on.

Hard Hearts!

Divorce is one of the worst examples of a hard heart because the cruelty is being done to the very one you have vowed to love. You will know if your heart is hardening toward your mate if you start keeping tabs on all the wrongs you have felt they have done. If you are doing this, I have some advice for you. Look in the mirror, you are the problem. Your heart is getting hard. You are not responsible and answerable to God for how another person treats you, but you will have to answer how you treat them.

Adultery and divorce cannot happen without one person in the marriage becoming hardened toward their spouse, and often time also to their children. I believe they also have hardened themselves against God.

Trading the Truth for a Lie

Another way people harden their hearts is they trade the truth of God for a lie. They chose to believe ridiculous theories of evolution and such garbage rather than to believe the truth. It gives them freedom to sin. Those who continue this way are given over to a reprobate mind.

God can clearly be seen in creation, those who chose to believe that everything that exists is an accident, have hardened their hearts.

For the wrath of God is revealed from heaven against all ungodliness and unrighteousness of men, who suppress the truth in unrighteousness, because what may be known of God is manifest in them, for God has shown it to them. For since the creation of the world His invisible attributes are clearly seen, being understood by the things that are made, even His eternal power and Godhead, so that they are without excuse, because, although they knew God, they did not glorify Him as God, nor were thankful, but became futile in their thoughts, and their foolish hearts were darkened. Romans1:18-21

Are you noticing that the words that go with hard hearts are words like God's wrath and judgement? We want to guard ourselves against our hearts becoming hard.

Bitterness Causes a Hard Heart

My daughter got a lesson on bitterness from the Holy Spirit. Joy was praying for people and blessing those as she prayed. Suddenly the Holy Spirit showed her someone's heart. This heart looked like an entangled mess of tree roots. It was totally closed off. The Holy Spirit explained to Joy that He could no longer enter this heart.

"Why?" Joy asked.

"Because of bitterness, these bitter roots have closed off this heart. I can no longer enter it."

Joy asked whose heart it was, and she was surprised it was a woman she knew from church.

We cannot allow bitterness to take root in our hearts and harden them.

Looking carefully lest anyone fall short of the grace of God; lest any root of bitterness springing up cause trouble, by this many become defiled; Hebrews 12:15

Hard hearts are stubborn, cold and unfeeling. Hard hearts are selfish and cruel. Hard hearts make us dead to God. We need to guard ourselves, stay alert and not to let our hearts get hard!

Chapter Thirteen

Tears

You number my wanderings;
Put my tears into your bottle Are they not in your
book?   *Psalms 56:8*

    I believe that tears, used in the proper way, are a key to keeping our broken hearts repaired.

    I feel qualified to write about tears because I have cried more than my share of tears. In the hardest times of my life, I took time to cry. I get alone with God when I cry. I want comfort from no one else. My tears are between me and God. They are like a prayer, an effective prayer. When I needed to cry, I would run to God, or sometimes just getting in God's presence would bring up my underlying tears.

    I remember the early years of my marriage I could keep up a good front until I got into church and started to worship. Then the tears would start to flow. I would cry all through church. My feelings I had managed to cover up, would come to the surface in His presence and then I would cry.

    There is a time to cry and there is a place to cry. The time to cry is when your heart has been broken, through trouble, through disappointment, grief or loss. The place to cry is before your Heavenly Father. Give your tears to Him.

There is no one else to whom your tears mean as much as your Father. He cherishes your tears; He bottles your tears, and He mixes your tears with His own. With the Father is the proper place to cry, the safe place to cry, and the place where it does the most good.

I have cried my tears with the Father so many times and something wonderful happens every time. He comforts me. He mends my broken heart. Over and over, I have been comforted by Him, and my heart goes from a place of inconsolable grief to a place of rest. He loves to comfort me. He loves to comfort us. He loves it when we run to Him.

Real Men Cry

There are some of you to whom I am writing, who need permission to cry. You have been taught not to cry. You have been taught wrong. You may cry. You may cry as long and as hard as you need to. You may cry until all your strength is gone. Real men may cry, just bring your tears to the Father.

I don't think we can find anyone tougher in the Bible than King David. I mean he was tough. He killed lions, he killed bears, and he killed giants. But he often cried. David knew the secret of bringing his tears to God. David said in Psalms; *I am weary of my groaning; All night I make my bed swim; I drench my couch with tears. Psalm 6:6*

Then later in chapter 6, David says;

For the Lord has heard the voice of my weeping. The Lord has heard my supplication; The Lord will receive my prayer. Psalm 6:8b-9 David went through much trouble in his life, but he also had great victories. I believe he held a key for men and women to follow.

The book of Samuel gives a good example of David weeping and the Lord answering his prayer dramatically. One time, when David and his men had returned to their home in Ziklag they found it had been raided by the Amalekites and burned and all their wives and children had been carried away. David took time to weep before the Lord.

Then David and the people who were with him lifted up their voices and wept, until they had no more power to weep. 1 Samuel 30:4 They sought the Lord, who instructed them to go after the Amalekites. On the way David and his men found a young man dying in the field, who just happened to be a servant of an Amalekite whom they had left behind because he has become ill. The young man led them to the Amalekites. A battle ensued and David won. The Bible tells us,

So David recovered all that the Amalekites had carried away, and David rescued his two wives. And nothing of theirs was lacking, either small or great, sons or daughters, spoil or anything which they had taken from them; David recovered all. 1 Samuel 30:16

David cried on the right shoulder. God led David and he recovered everything. I believe David's tears moved the giant heart of God.

I remember one particular time when I was very angry and hurt with my husband after he had started drinking again. I just never got used to it. I asked my brother in law Walter to pray for me. As he started to pray for me, I felt the Holy Spirit very strongly. The Holy Spirit came up on the inside of me and pushed out my hurt. I started wailing. I felt a push from the inside of me as the sobs and tears came out with force. It only lasted a minute or two and then up came laughter and joy. I laughed and laughed; I felt such freedom from the hurt that minutes before was devastating me. I felt light as a feather.

I realized the Holy Spirit was helping me cry, and once I cried all the hurt and pain went up and out. I believe that bringing my tears to God has kept my heart stay healed. But for many years' tears were a daily part of my life.

Tears Bear Fruit

Those who sow in tears shall reap in joy. He who continually goes forth weeping, bearing seed for sowing, shall doubtless come again with rejoicing, bringing his sheaves with him. Psalm 126:5-6

Blessed are you who weep now, for you shall laugh, Luke 6:21b

Tears bring forth fruit. Tears are a sincere showing of what is in our hearts and when offered to God they bring forth a response from Him. They never go unnoticed.

I wrote in my book, *What Can I do for God?* about my desert and how God did not waste my tears. All the years I had spent crying, sometimes daily and praying for the things in my life to change I saw myself in a desert. It was a real place. This desert seemed to go on forever and I was crossing it for so many years. I would weep as I crossed it, wondering if things were hopeless for my family. I wondered if my children would survive the chaos we were going through, I wondered if the chaos would ever end. Sometimes things would seem better for a while, and I would think maybe I was coming to the end of my desert.

This particular day as I wept before the Lord was like that, I had thought maybe things had changed but here I was back in the desert and weeping again. I tried to look ahead and see if the end of the desert was ahead, and then I did something I had never done before, in all those years. I turned around and looked behind me, to see the desert I had already crossed.

I gasped in amazement.

There was no desert behind me. As far as I could see was lush beautiful scenery. It looked more like a garden.

"Lord," I gasped, "Where is the desert?"

"Summer," the Lord answered, "It is a garden now you have watered the desert with your tears."

Our tears bear fruit! The tears I had cried for my life, at the time seemingly wasted, I had produced a garden of fruit, fruit of love and forgiveness and beauty. The tears I had cried for my children had blossomed into beauty, they were not destroyed they were overcomers. I sowed with tears, but I reaped in joy. God did not waste my tears but produced a garden in the desert.

Jesus Wept

The Bible tells us that Jesus wept. He wept at the tomb of His friend Lazarus. Jesus knew full well that He was going to raise Lazarus from the dead; He had told His disciples on the way. And yet Jesus still took the time to weep. He wept to the point that the people present exclaimed, "See how He loved him!"

Now I can't give you a reason why Jesus stopped and took time to cry when He knew he was going to raise Lazarus from the dead except that maybe, His tears were His prayer. It certainly brings across the importance of tears that Jesus took time to cry.

Tears are an integral part of our emotional healing. They are also an effective way to pray. Prayers do not always require words. Feelings, emotions, tears and pictures lifted up to God will do. In heaven people do not always communicate with words, they communicate with thought and emotion. You can start doing this now by lifting your grief and tears as a prayer to the Lord. I can guarantee you this; He will hear you loud and clear! Jesus did this, King David did this, and you can do this too.

Chapter Fourteen

The Beauty of Brokenness

And He said to me, "My grace is sufficient for you, for My strength is made perfect in weakness." Therefore, most gladly I will rather boast in my infirmities, that the power of Christ may rest upon me. Therefore, I take pleasure in infirmities, in reproaches, in needs, in persecutions, in distresses, for Christ's sake. For when I am weak, then I am strong.
    2 Corinthians 12:9-10

If God is God, why does He let abuse happen? Why does He stand back and let us be broken? Why doesn't He do something? Is it His will that people are abused?

No, absolutely not.

But, yes, He does let it happen; and He will take what has been broken and make something beautiful from it.

There is a Japanese art which is done using broken pieces of pottery called Kintsugi. Kintsugi is an art which fuses broken pottery back together with gold. Kintsugi comes from the word kintsukori which literally means to repair with gold.

This art takes something that is broken, {pottery} and makes it into something that is much more beautiful than it was at the beginning. Now it is something much more valuable than just a bowl or a plate or a vase, it is a beautiful work of art. It has a much higher value and a much higher purpose.

This is similar to us. God takes the pieces of our broken hearts and fuses them back together with gold! The gold is Him. Now we are no longer common and ordinary. We have become a beautiful piece of artwork. We have a higher value, and we have a higher purpose. We become strong in our broken places. We become strong in our weaknesses; those become the places in us that are filled in with Christ.

I was looking at the pictures of the kintsugi before I began this chapter, and I noticed something. First of all, each piece was very beautiful. Some pieces only had one or two broken places, so they had gold infused in their cracks and were beautiful, but the most beautiful pieces were the pieces that had many broken places. They were filled with a lot of gold. They were extremely beautiful. The more broken places the more beautiful was the end result.

We have to offer our broken hearts to God. He will fuse us back together with gold and the end result is beautiful. We become strong in our broken places. That is where His power is made perfect, in our weaknesses.

The Bottom of the Pecking Order

I remember sitting in church one Sunday many years ago and hearing the pastor say there is a pecking order in the church and there is also a pecking order in heaven. His statement depressed me. I felt so broken for so long. I didn't just feel that way just about myself but my husband and children also. I would sit in church and think we will always be on the bottom, not only on earth but in heaven also. I would see the pastor of the church ministering and the elders praying for people and think we could never be like that. In fact, we always needed some kind of help. We frequently needed food. If our car broke down, we could not take it to a mechanic, we could not afford one. Jim would have to find someone who could help him put the part on. And it was not just money problems either. Our home was often in an uproar.

So, I would think to myself, "We will be on the bottom in heaven also, we are the lowest of the low, no one would ever consider having us to have any importance in the church."

And truthfully, churches can't have broken people in any kind of ministry position, can they?

But I was wrong. I did not yet understand how marvelous God is, especially to us broken people. He wants us. His heart is moved toward us. And He does not ever judge us by the condition we are in. He has this incredible way of judgement that is not bad it is good. He judges us not on what a mess we are but on how hard we are trying. And even if we fail, over and over and over again to be the kind of person we think we should be, the fact that we still keep trying against all odds puts us not on the bottom of His pecking order but on the top. And if we never stop trying.....we never stop moving up.

This took me so long to figure out because I kept thinking I have never accomplished anything. I did not have any souls won to the Lord or any big thing that I had done for God. In fact, I was just a blob of nothing on the earth. I wasn't accomplishing anything. {I wrote about this in my book, *What Can I do for God?}*

I knew both Jim and I were too big of a mess to ever be used by God, so I kept up a really good front. I tried to hide the real us and convince people that we had it all together. I tried for years to hide our brokenness. If the yelling broke out, I would run around and close the windows and curtains hoping neighbors wouldn't hear.

My worst moments were if Jim should get riled up in a grocery store or some other public place, then there was nowhere to hide. It was the deepest of humilities.

One time Jim showed up drunk at my workplace. My horror knew no bounds. My goody two shoes front was uncovered. The look of horror on my face pressed Jim's rejection button and he started his yelling and cussing at me in front of my coworkers. No matter how hard I tried to hide what we were, I just couldn't seem to, but it didn't stop me from trying.

I wanted some respectability. I wanted us to look like good Christians. I wanted us to be good Christians. I wanted for God to someday use us, but we were just too broken. I kept hoping we could get good enough, but years went by, and it seemed to be too late.

Then God told me to write a book about my marriage. I had a problem; I had been trying to hide this stuff from the world. I walked around with a pencil and a notebook for over a year, nothing got written.

For years I had tried to pull together some goodness and holiness, but that is not what God wanted to use. He wanted to use our brokenness. He wanted to use our weaknesses and our failures, the things we had struggled with our whole lives and yes, we gained ground, but we still had such a long way to go. How could I write this stuff?

I was hoping that no one that we knew would read it,

maybe God could use it in China or something. But that was not the case. Although we didn't sell that many books, the book was more successful than I possibly could have imagined. It was successful in a different way. We found our story ministered to people. I was astounded.

Our strength was in our weakness, this is where God's grace is, this is where the broken pottery of our lives has been fused together with gold. He has made beauty from our brokenness.

Jesus Was Broken

The Lord Jesus on the night he was betrayed took bread, and when He had given thanks, He broke it and said, "This is my body, which is for you; do this in remembrance of Me." 1Corinthians 11:23

Why is a man's torture and death on a cross so holy and so beautiful to me? Why has it become the center of my life? Why has something so gruesome become so holy to me that I can only think of it in an attitude of awe and wonder?

The brokenness of Jesus is beautiful, incredibly beautiful.

But why?

Because it is our worth.

We had become worthless because of sin. Our value had been lost. Our worth, which had now become nothing, is reestablished by the price that was paid for us.

What did God pay for us? How much?

He paid all that He had for us. Jesus is the Father's wealth; He is His heart and soul. And Jesus paid all that He had, including every drop of blood.

Our worth is incredible, it goes beyond money or things, and it goes beyond comprehension. The brokenness of Jesus is beautiful, it is our worth.

But there is something more to look at. There is a beauty that can only be released through suffering. Because in a universe where love is the highest and greatest and most valuable thing to be desired, this is the ultimate test.

Love is unique. It is not something that can be forced. We cannot force someone to love us. We cannot demand it. It has to be willingly given. To love someone is to take a risk. You do not know if your love will be returned. It makes us vulnerable. Many have been hurt this way. Betrayal by a spouse is the worst kind of pain. So, love must be freely given.

Love can also be tested. We stand at the altar and promise to love our spouse, but when testing comes many leave. Sickness may come, temptation may come, and our spouse may have problems we do not want to deal with. It is easy to love someone when they are lovable, but how about when they are not? How many times have we seen it happen? The spouse becomes sick and the one who vowed to love until death leaves. Or how many times have we seen the total opposite, the one who loves regardless of what happens, until death. Our love will be tested. Will we pass the test? It is a true test of worth, because love is the most important test to pass.

Jesus passed this test. His love was tested beyond endurance and yet He passed this test. He not only proved His love for us, He proved His love for the Father. He proved it through suffering, agony, torture and pain. Love required Jesus to be broken. He did not run when love required Him to face, a cross, death and hell. Unbelievable good was released, beauty was released, power was released, and mankind was released from death. Love has to be proved through suffering.

The greatest in the eternal realm are those who have

proved their love. They have faced their own tests and trials and passed. This why martyrs hold such a high honor and will also remain on earth during the Millennium. They have proved their love with their life.

Our lives on earth are a test. Do you see now why God allows suffering? But it won't be for long, He will end all that soon. Then the time for promotion will have passed. We have an opportunity that will not come around again. It is the same opportunity that Jesus had, and He passed with flying colors. And that is the opportunity to face the suffering in our life in such a way that we may prove our love not only to the people God has placed in it, but also to prove our love for God Himself.

Chapter Fifteen

Does Life Stink?

Do not be overcome by evil but overcome evil with good. Romans 12:21

When I try to describe the state, I was in it becomes difficult. I keep saying I was a mess, and I had no personality and that was true, but when I was comfortable and I did come out of my shell, I was spoiled, manipulative, prideful, selfish and very self-centered. There did not seem much good about me.

When I got married to Jim, I jumped out of the frying pan and into the fire. I could not handle life before and now my life was totally out of control and a complete mess, inside and out. Needless to say, for many years' life just plain stunk. It was hard, hard, hard.

I loved Jim, sometimes, but he was so out of control

and scary I also hated him. He was also my tormentor. I was swinging constantly on a pendulum between love and hate, depending on his behavior which was usually awful.

I mean really awful. The Michigan Department of Corrections had a classification for their inmates. They graded them according to how dangerous they were. Jim, who had been in their system almost his whole life, had the highest rating, one of the qualifications being having committed his first felony before the age of fourteen. When Jim was incarcerated, he always was kept in maximum security. There was a reason for this. He could be like a wild animal, he was scary, especially when he drank, which was a lot! If the Department of Corrections could not handle him and they had armed guards and cells and bars, what was I going to do???!!!

I used to have this fantasy in my mind that I had a cell I could lock Jim up and keep him in it when he got on a rampage. Then I could go to sleep and let him out when he settled down. But I did not have a cage and I went through hell, which would go on for hours, many, many nights.

Of course, you can imagine that I would think that I missed God somewhere I wasn't supposed to marry Jim, everybody else I knew thought this.

Why would God put this broken person that I was, in this situation? Was all my life ever going to be, pain and agony and trouble and brokenness?

It seemed that way for many years but that was not so. You see I have been married almost 37 years now and I now have some perspective.

Something wonderful happened!

God was in this, after all.

I entered into this marriage broken and shattered but I have come out on the other side a different person, a healed person, and not just me, both of us, Jim and me.

A miracle has taken place inside of me. {Not that I am finished yet, far from it, but I am so much better.}

So, what happened?

Well, at first my response to Jim, would be, poor, poor pitiful me, my typical response to everything. And that Jim was a big meany. But God had to get me, to get my eyes off myself. It took many years. He would show me over and over that I was not the victim, Jim was. That yes, I was in much pain, and yes it did seemingly come from Jim, but, no, that wasn't really the case here. Even though, abusive things were happening through Jim they were not being done by Jim. They were being done by Jim's enemies, which were inside of him. They were the two other personalities, which were demonic, that had developed within him, and were stronger than his own. I had to see that the Jim that was tormenting me was not the real Jim. I had to see the invisible, like God does. And I had to love and forgive, over and over.

This did not happen overnight. This took years. And at first, I only saw through a glass dimly, very dimly. Over and over, He had to show me.

Frequently God would show me in my dreams. I dreamt of giants that would overpower Jim and come after me. The giants were the demonic forces that would overpower Jim. Then I would realize that it was the giants causing me pain and not Jim.

This especially helped me when our son entered his teen years, if it had not been for the dream that came first warning me, I may not have been able to handle what happened.

Jim and our son Jamie have always been very close. It was Jim's happiest day when Jamie was born. He immediately bonded and they did everything together from day one. But Jamie has also suffered the most because of his dysfunctional parents. Jim even with all his problems, was a wonderful dad to Jamie. His dad loved him and spent much time with him.

When Jamie hit his teen years, I had a dream, a nightmare. I dreamt Jamie was in the water and he was drowning. He was screaming. Jim heard him and ran to the edge of the water to save Jamie but just as Jim got to the water, one of the giants blocked him and Jim could not get to Jamie.

This giant was the spirit of addiction and when it attacked Jamie, Jim could not help him. I don't think our marriage could have survived this point if I had not had this understanding. Even so it was hard enough.

The things God would show me were not always heavy, sometimes it was fun. God could make it fun. I remember one time I was in church, and a famous woman evangelist came to speak. She told everyone to line up and she was going to come and pray for us and when she did, we were to get quiet, and God was going to tell us a secret. Well, we all lined up and she prayed and most of us fell on the floor when she prayed, me included. As I was lying there on the floor wondering if God was really going to say something to me, I heard Him whisper. He said, "Jim's true personality is very gentle."

I laid there and laughed and laughed. My aggressive, bully, of a husband was very gentle. It was funny to me, but it was a very happy thought, and I knew it was true, it was his very gentle side that attracted me to him in the first place, it was just that I rarely saw it anymore. But now, years later I rarely see him aggressive. Jim's true personality has developed.

This work in me happened between me and God. I realized slowly that it was not about me and my pain. God had to show me this over and over. He acknowledged my pain, that I felt Jim was putting me through, but He showed me Jim was the one in real pain. Jim was the real target. I was only getting a small portion being near Jim.

Oh, those demonic personalities were targeting me; they wanted me out of the way. I was a real threat to them. They wanted me to hate Jim and get revenge and hurt him. And many times, they succeeded. And then God would open my eyes again.

Can you imagine, fearful, self-centered me, asking my drinking, seemingly abusive husband to forgive me and then loving and forgiving him and accepting him just as he is? God was doing a work in me. A huge work, I was facing my fears, I was not just selfishly thinking about myself anymore, I was in a very small way becoming like Jesus, I was learning to love.

Remember what Jesus told my daughter, Joy in chapter 2. Jesus was totally shattered. His heart was in a million pieces. He was lying in torment in the lowest pit of hell having endured days of beatings, scourging, being spit on, laughed at stripped and mocked, his beard pulled out and finally crucified. Then being handed over to the host of hell who had come together in their hatred of Him and unleashed their fury in hell. Then as He lay there in hell, the lowest pit, His heart was shattered, as He told Joy, but, every piece of His broken heart loved us. He did not make it about Him, it was about us. He is Love pure Love.

Love is the most powerful force in the universe, nothing can touch it, and no evil can oppose it and overpower it. God's love looks like light, blinding light, which dispels darkness and hate and evil. It also flows out of

Him like a River; a River from His innermost being that heals all who come to it. This River is life to our broken hearts. We need to let it flow through us. As it flows from God through us it will heal us and heal others too.

The highest goal and calling and meaning in life is to become more like Jesus. In order to understand this, we have to understand what Jesus is like and the answer to that is love. He chose, out of love for us, to face what He did face, and He did this for the very ones whose sins nailed Him to the cross. And on the cross, He implored God to forgive the ones who crucified Him.

Love and forgive, love and forgive, love and forgive, this is Jesus; and this was what Jesus was trying to teach me.

I have lived through marriage to an alcoholic who is an ex-convict. But I don't need any healing for the hard years I have been through. They were my healing. God used walking with Him and learning to love and forgive someone else to heal my broken heart. That was my healing.

Through my marriage God taught me to love. Not just to love, Jim, my husband, but also to love God. But it goes even deeper than that. I have learned to love something else, actually two other things. Two things that were so ugly and so repulsive to me that I did not think I could ever love them, and maybe I am not even sure I do now, But I think I am starting to.

Those two things are myself and living.

Chapter Sixteen

Authority to Minister

And our hope is steadfast, because we know that as you are partakers of the sufferings, so also you will partake of the consolation. 2 Corinthians1:7

Authority is a big deal not only in our physical world but even much more in the spiritual world. Legal authority means you have a right to do what you are doing. Using illegal authority means trouble. What would happen in the army if a private started giving orders to a general? I don't know because I doubt anyone has ever been that crazy. It would be just as drastic in the spirit realm.

There are levels of authority in place in the spirit world. Satan has authority over the earth for a time. He received it from Adam who had been given authority. He has rulers set in place all over the world. Over geographical areas and also over people who have allowed them access. They, the devil and his cohorts know they have authority and there is constant haggling over legal matters in the courtrooms of heaven.

Jesus overcame Satan and death and hell. We are

now in transition. The earth will be regained through the sons of God, which is us. But there is a price to be paid.

There have been times we have prayed against demons that refuse to leave because they have a legal right to be there. The person has allowed the evil spirit access and the spirit won't leave. Some ways that people allow legal access to devils is by sin, their words, frequenting places of evil or working in them, drugs, alcohol, illicit sex, possessing objects dedicated to evil practices etc. In order for that person to obtain deliverance they have to correct the problem by renouncing the evil deed, repentance or removing an object from their possession.

Those who place themselves under Jesus' authority have been translated out of Satan's authority, out of his kingdom of darkness, and are now under authority in the kingdom of light.

God is not a giant dictator playing with our lives like we were puppets. Everything is done legally, and God follows the laws also even though He is the Supreme Authority. Each of us has been delegated some authority by God, that we are responsible for, and we are answerable for. We are answerable for how we treat those God places in our lives.

God has delegated to us something precious, the right to choose our own destiny. He has given us a free will. We can choose whom we will serve. Not only can we choose God, we can also decide our own level in heaven, through the way we live our life on earth. We can be as close to God as we want to be. If we pay the price to draw close to Him, He will draw close to us. Real destinies are being decided on earth, the choice to choose or reject God and to spend eternity in heaven or hell and our places and positions for eternity. Life is serious business.

Some human beings are using their freedom to choose, and they are choosing evil, and they are hurting other people. They steal, kill, rape and abuse other human beings. These things can never be undone and there is a real hell they will enter unless they repent. The stakes of life are very high.

What about their victims, what about those who are hurt? They also have a choice. They can be overcome by evil, or they can overcome evil with good. They can become part of the world's problems or part of the answer. Those who overcome receive a higher level of authority. They receive the authority to minister in the very area they were wounded.

All evil is ultimately inspired by the devil and his cohorts. There are two victims in every crime, the person who succumbs to the devil's temptation and the victim of the crime. I have many times seen the victim of the crime not only overcome the enemy for themselves but also for the person who hurt them, by responding correctly to the situation, the way Jesus taught us to respond.

I read a story in an article which is a perfect example. The article described a young man named Anthony Colon whose unarmed brother Wilfredo was gunned down; he was shot thirteen times. Anthony became filled with hate and rage and missed his brother terribly. Later in life Anthony married and became a Christian. His attitude toward his brother's killers changed. He forgave.

One day while Anthony was visiting a friend in prison, he looked across the room and saw one of his brother's killers, a man named Michael Rowe.

Michael saw Anthony also and tried to duck out of sight, but it was too late. Anthony walked straight over to Michael. Michael expected a fight but was surprised when

Anthony said to him, "Brother, I have been praying for you. I forgave you. I have been praying I would see you again."

The meeting transformed both men's lives. Michael had been eaten up with guilt. Now he was forgiven. Anthony visited Michael in prison. Soon Michael became involved with an organization called Exodus, which helps men prepare for their release. Through Exodus, Michael received his bachelor's degree in prison and Anthony was there for his graduation. He was also there when he appeared before the parole board and after twenty years in prison was released from prison. Now both men work together at Exodus, in a program that reaches out to young men at risk.

Michael says of Anthony, "Anthony is my hero. I have two sons and if my sons grow up to be half the man that Anthony Colon is, I will be an incredibly proud father. And I don't know if I can sum it up or explain any better about Anthony Colon. He has changed my life."

Anthony defeated the devil in this situation and gained spiritual authority. Anthony also was able break the devil's power over Michael the very one who killed his brother. Anthony followed the example of Jesus, to win this victory. {Love and forgive, love and forgive.} Now he has a higher place than he used to, a higher level of authority, he is ministering to young men at risk through a program called Exodus, but not just Anthony also Michael. Both of these men have overcome the enemy. They will be effective in their work because they have gained authority over the enemy.

Jesus gained authority over the enemy also. Jesus had authority over Satan, but we did not. We were legal captives. Jesus came to earth as a human and defeated Satan for us. There is a reason His punishment was so harsh, it was because of His high calling, the highest calling. He had to go to the lowest hell but then He was given the highest place. Let's look at some scripture.{*Now this, "he ascended"- what does it mean but that He also first descended into the lower parts of the earth? He who descended is also the One who ascended far above all the heavens, that He might fill all things.} Ephesians 4:9-10*

Let this mind be in you which was also in Christ Jesus, who being in the form of God, did not consider it robbery to be equal with God, but made Himself of no reputation, taking the form of a bond-servant, and coming in the likeness of men. And being found in appearance as a man, he humbled Himself and became obedient to the point of death, even the death of the cross. Therefore God also has highly exalted Him and given Him the name which is above every name, that at the name of Jesus every knee should bow, of those in heaven, and those of earth, and those under the earth, and that every tongue should confess that Jesus Christ is Lord, to the glory of God the Father. Philippians 2:5-11

Jesus gained authority by His suffering. He defeated evil and He gained the highest place, but first He went to the lowest place and overcame the enemy. He literally went to the lowest pit in hell.

He also left us an example to defeat Satan the same way, by overcoming evil with good. I want to quote a passage from the book, The Final Quest, by Rick Joyner. The passage is on this very subject. No one anywhere could say it any better.

"God has a different definition of peace and safety than we do. To be wounded in the fight is a great honor. It is by the Lord's stripes we are healed, and it is through our stripes that we, too, are given the authority for healing. In the very place that the enemy wounds us, once we are healed, we are given the power to heal

others. Healing was a basic part of the Lord's ministry, and it is also a basic part of ours. That is one reason why the Lord allows bad things to happen to His people, so that they can receive the compassion for others by which the power of healing operates. That is why the apostle Paul told of his beatings and stoning's when his authority was questioned. Every wound, every bad thing that happens to us can be turned into the authority to do good. Every beating that the great apostle took resulted in salvation for others. Every wound that every warrior takes will result in others being, saved healed or restored."

In this paragraph is the answer to a question that has caused many people to stumble. Why does God allow bad things to happen to His people? There is something gained through suffering, something eternal and something that is not easily understood at this time. Authority.

There are eons to come, an eternity of existence in realms not yet known. Oh, we have a little glimpse at the end of the Book of Revelation. There is a huge universe out there, with many worlds; the New Jerusalem on earth will be the capital of that universe. God is now preparing those who will rule with Him for eternity, an honor beyond imagination. He is preparing them now through suffering. He is testing them. The stakes are very high. {This is what Paul was talking about. For I consider that the sufferings of this present time are not worthy to be compared with the glory which will be revealed in us, Romans 8:18}

I want to quote one more section, of, The Final Quest, which talks about our scars being our medals of honor in heaven.

"These scars are the glory that we will carry forever. That is why even the wounds our Lord suffered

are with Him in heaven. You can still see His wounds and the wounds that all of His chosen ones have taken for His sake. These are the medals of honor in heaven. All who carry them love God and His truth more than their own lives. These are the ones who followed the Lamb wherever He went, being willing to suffer for the sake of truth, righteousness and salvation of men. True leaders of His people, who carry genuine authority, must have first proven their devotion this way."

Authority to minister comes through what we have been through and have been healed of. In the very places we have been wounded we have the ability to heal others. As Jesus did, when we have overcome the enemy, then we have gained authority.

The things we suffer are opportunities for advancement. Those who have suffered much, have much to gain.

This makes me think of Joyce Meyer, a woman with a great and powerful ministry. Joyce has a powerful testimony of overcoming evil with good.

Joyce grew up in an abusive home. Her father molested her for years while her mother looked the other way. She longed for a way out but found none until she became old enough to marry and married to get away from her father. She entered her adult life, a Christian, but broken and angry and a mess.

After her first marriage failed God brought Joyce her husband Dave. Dave was Joyce's rock. God used Dave and Joyce's marriage to help bring healing to Joyce. With God's help Joyce has overcome the enemy that tried to destroy her life. She was even able to lead her father who abused her to the Lord. It was not easy, but God led her one step at a time.

Her ministry is birthed out of the authority received

through her suffering. Joyce is very brave to candidly tell her story. Joyce's suffering has led to many others being saved, healed and delivered.

Joyce's ministry is so powerful, one friend of mine told me, "When I listen to Joyce Meyer, I get healed of problems I did not even realize that I had."

Nobody wants to suffer, but suffering can lead us to a higher level of authority. The key is to follow Jesus example and overcome evil with good. We do not do this alone. Jesus blazed this trail for us, and Jesus goes with us. We do this in His strength. We do this His way, the way He has treated us and the way He wants us to treat others, love and forgive, love and forgive, love and forgive. This is the way we overcome evil with good.

Chapter Seventeen

Staying Filled with Oil

*"The kingdom of heaven shall be likened to ten virgins
who took their lamps and went out to meet the bridegroom.
Now five of them were wise and five were foolish. Those who
were foolish took their lamps and took no oil with them, but
the wise took oil in their vessels with their lamps. But while
the bridegroom was delayed, they all slumbered and slept.
And at midnight a cry was heard:' Behold the bridegroom is
coming go out and meet him!' Then all those virgins arose and
trimmed their lamps. And the foolish said to the wise, 'Give us
some of your oil, for our lamps are going out.' But the wise
answered saying,' No lest there should not be enough for us
and you; but go rather to those who sell and buy for
yourselves.' And while they went to buy, the bridegroom came,
and those who were ready went in with him to the wedding;
and the door was shut. Afterward the other virgins came also,
saying, 'Lord, Lord, open to us!" But he answered and said,
'Assuredly, I say to you, I do not know you.' Watch therefore,
for you know neither the day nor the hour in which the son of*

man is coming." Matthew 25:1-13

My dad has managed to drill it into Jim and I that if we want to keep our cars running that we have to keep up with the oil maintenance. Jim has a close relationship with our service center. He is there every three months with both cars, and he stops in two times in-between for top offs. If you don't keep oil in your car something awful will happen, I'm not quite sure what but I am not going to find out.

Our spirit also needs maintenance. We are supposed to stay filled with oil also. We are supposed to stay filled up. This is heart maintenance. We learn about this in a parable Jesus talked about the ten virgins, five wise and the five foolish virgins.

It is very foolish to be caught without oil and wise to have a supply. Oil stands for the Holy Spirit, and it stands for anointing, and it also stands for unity. The way to be ready spiritually is to have a supply of oil.

My daughter Joy recently had a dream. She said it was actually it was a bad dream, but Jesus appeared in it. At first, she did not know who He was, but she knew He was good. His face was beautiful. But he was dressed in a uniform with a name tag which said Phillip.

She asked Him, Are you an angel?"

"No,' he answered.

"Are you Jesus?"

"Yes."

"But why does you tag say Phillip?" Joy asked.

"Because you need to fill up, "Jesus told her.

Joy was running on empty spiritually, and Jesus was reminding her of her need.

We fill up with Jesus. We fill up full of His Holy Spirit. The Bible gives us plenty of instructions on how to do this.

Therefore, do not be unwise, but understand what the

will of the Lord is. And do not be drunk with wine, in which is dissipation, but be filled with the Spirit, speaking to one another in psalms and hymns and spiritual songs, singing and making melody in your heart to the Lord, giving thanks always for all things to God the Father in the name of the Lord Jesus Christ, submitting to one another in the fear of God. Ephesians 5:17-21

Notice the exhortation to not be unwise but be filled with the spirit. Then we receive some practical advice on singing and being thankful. This is fill up advice. The advice is for a continual singing and meditating on praise to the Lord. The New Testament is full of fill up advice. Here's another.

But you, beloved, building yourselves up in the most holy faith, praying in the Holy Spirit, keep yourself in the love of God, looking for the mercy of our Lord Jesus Christ unto eternal life. Jude 1:20

This is more fill up instructions. Praying in tongues is filling up and building up your spirit man. And we can keep the praying in the spirit going all day too.

Here is another Psalm 1, *Blessed is the man who walks not in the counsel of the ungodly, Nor stands in the path of sinners, Nor sits in the seat of the scornful; But his delight is in the law of the Lord, And on His law he meditates day and night. He shall be like a tree planted by the rivers of water, that brings forth its fruit in season, whose leaf shall not wither, and whatever he does shall prosper. Psalm 1:1-3*

Meditating on the Word of God is terrific fill up advice. There is more, fellowshipping with the Lord, gratitude, thinking on good things, casting your care on the Lord, praying without ceasing, rejoicing in the Lord always, the Bible is full of ways to fill up. Jesus even said to His disciples when they worried about Him being hungry His food was to do the will of the Father.

Let's keep full of oil, this is heart maintenance. Let's not be like the foolish virgins who ran out of oil. Let's be wise and be ready.

Chapter Eighteen

Restoration

A certain man went down from Jerusalem to Jericho, and fell among thieves, who stripped him of his clothing, wounded him and departed, leaving him half dead. Now by chance a certain priest came down that road. And when he saw him, he passed by on the other side. Likewise, a Levite, when he arrived at the place, came and looked, and passed by on the other side. But a certain Samaritan as he journeyed, came where he was. And when he saw him, he had compassion. So, he went to him, and bandaged his wounds, pouring on oil and wine; and he set him on his own animal, brought him to an inn, and took care of him. On the next day, when he departed, he took out two denarii, gave them to the innkeeper, and said to him, 'Take care of him and whatever more you spend, when I come again, I will repay you." Luke 10:30-35

When I hear the word restoration I think of my son. I have had the hardest time starting this chapter. I didn't want to write this chapter because I did not want to make anyone look bad. It is hard when someone hurts one of your children, not to despise them. The truth is I don't, but that took some struggle. And now I have to tell the story, but I don't want to do it in any way to hurt those who have hurt my son. So, I am going to try to walk on eggshells here and not go into a lot of detail, but I want you the reader to benefit.

This story is about my son, James. I call him Jay. He is my hero. I have seen this kid make it against all odds. He had learning disabilities which really showed up in first grade when it was time to read and write. He flunked first grade; in fact, he flunked every grade in school, but they just kept moving him up rather than dealing with him. I never saw anyone work so hard. His sisters would come home from school and play, and Jay would face frustration all night long trying to do the work he couldn't get done in school and he would still fail.

Jay is my hero because he never gave up. He kept plugging away until it was time to graduate and then he took adult classes and got a GED. Then somehow and I don't know how, it was a miracle, he went to college and got a bachelor's degree, while supporting his family.

Jay had more than his share of struggles in his life, growing up in an alcoholic home and then his learning disabilities but the worst was yet to come. This is why I have to tell his story. It seemed after all Jay's hard work that his life had really come together. He had a wife he loved and two children. He had finished college and had a job and also worked in ministry. He had been a youth pastor all the years of college and now he had come back to his hometown and was the youth pastor at our home church.

Jay is incredible. He is so much fun. I always think he could have made it as a stand-up comic he has that kind of personality. He is fun looking for a place to happen, but more than that, he loves people. I thought his future looked bright.

Jay lost everything. I mean everything. It started with

115

his wife. You know the story it had happened to many marriages, she connected with her old boyfriend online. There was a lot of deception going on and while he was hoping for reconciliation and allowed her to move with the kids, she was just planning on getting away with the kids to where the boyfriend was.

He was like a lamb led to the slaughter and he got slaughtered, over and over again. He was trying to give love and understanding, and he got a knife twisted in his back. When I say he lost everything, his family, his friends, his ministry, he lost his income, his possessions.

First, she just took what she wanted the stuff of value, the computer, the car; she left the household items with him. Without income, he had to move so we all, mom and dad and aunt and uncle, helped him pack up the furniture and everything left and move him into an apartment in my basement. It was a big job.

After we got everything done, she decided she wanted a few more things. Jay told me her parents were going to come and pick up some things later that day. I had a bad feeling about it, but I had to go to work. I quickly grabbed his vacuum cleaner and a box of garbage bags he had just bought and put them upstairs. My feeling was correct. His in-laws whom he loved and trusted showed up in a moving van. They walked in and gave him a hug and kiss and then they took everything he owned.

He came up in shock. He said he was going to set up his household, but everything was gone. At least he had garbage bags and a vacuum cleaner. But that is not what hurt. What hurt was that Jay's kids were four hours away. He couldn't see them every day.

If things could get worse, they got worse. Jay became clinically depressed, and his health wasn't good. He lost a lot

116

of weight. The shock even affected his health, and at one point he was hospitalized.

He was out of work for a couple of months and then he took a low paying job which was a good decision because his employer was flexible. He was able to spend time with his kids when he had them, he could leave if they got sick or needed him.

Another problem was the divorce proceedings were four hours away, and his ex-wife was claiming he was making more than he was and that she was making nothing, neither was true and he wasn't there to straighten things out, so more than half his income went to child support. Can you imagine working hard only to have no money?

Nothing seemed to work out for Jay. During this time, he tried out for a play at the local community theatre. He wanted to do something positive, I thought he would have been perfect for the part, but it is very hard to get those parts, you kind of have to be known. But still it would have been nice, Jay had been in lots of church plays, and he was always a hit in those. Like everything in his life at that time he was rejected. His life just seemed to be going down.

I wondered how God could let this happen. I hoped things would get better, but they didn't seem to. My grandchildren were suffering, and my son was ground to dust. I prayed endlessly. I started to feel like God didn't love my son as much as I did. If He did, would He let this happen? I was trying not to feel this way, but I did.

God dealt with my hidden thoughts in a powerful way. He finally spoke up. He passionately spoke of how much he loved Jay. He told me, "You do not have to convince Me to love My son, I love him."

Then He likened the situation to the story of the Good Samaritan. He said that Satan had beaten up and robbed Jay and as he lay dying on the side of the road many passed him by. "But" the Lord said, "I have picked him up and brought him to my Father's Inn. I have lain on my face before My Father, and I have paid for him."

This was something God was going to do personally, and He let me know it, He was not going to leave Jay, He was going to restore his life. His big heart was moved! I was ashamed that I had doubted His love for Jay.

I also had a dream about my son at this time, which I did not understand As I was in the car driving to work and I was praying about the dream a truck drove by with the word RESTORE painted on the side. The Lord said, "That is what the dream means, I will restore Jay's life."

Jay had a girlfriend for a short time but he didn't like the way she treated his kids so that was over, and he did not even date. He lived for his children. And in his mind things got better much better. His ex-wife moved back to town, and he got his children almost half of the time. This made Jay very happy. He seemed happy but I was not.

I saw him being twisted like a pretzel at someone else's expense. It seemed to me everything was for his ex-wife's benefit. The kids had the school bus from her house to school, but Jay had to drive them to school and back. He had them whenever she had somewhere to go so, she never had to pay for a babysitter, but Jay did this gladly.

Jay had them in the summers and had the burden of providing babysitters and food and keeping them busy. He had every responsibility as if he were a full-time parent, he had bedrooms and beds and a home for them, he bought them their clothes, shoes, coats etc. Whatever they needed he found a way to provide it was his joy.

But it did not seem fair to me she got school lunches supplied and all the tax help, but meanwhile Jay was paying into her household, but he had just as much responsibility if not more. He usually had them on weekends, got no break on child support or a tax exemption and he even had to pay taxes on the child support. {Not fair IRS} And because some of his income was self-employment every year his tax bill was growing. He was growing in debt every year with the IRS and the fines and interest were growing. This disturbed me.

Years went by.

I wondered if things would ever change.

I have to tell you something about this incredible son of mine. Everything he went through; he never became bitter. He was angry for a while, he suffered depression, but he never became bitter and even though his situation especially financially was bleak, he still enjoyed his life. He has enjoyed every moment of being a parent. In fact, he is the best parent I have ever seen, and I am not just saying that because he is my son.

Jay has a son, named Kellan and a daughter, named Mikaila. His son was four almost five and his daughter was two almost three when all this happened. Jay has enjoyed being a dad. His circumstances never soured him. For eight years they stayed in my home, and I watched Jay enjoy them. Every minute with them was precious to him. He has lived a happy, joyful life despite of his circumstances, because of his love and appreciation for his children.

Jay would throw the kids big parties on their birthdays and have all their friends from school. In fact, he kept track of who their friends are, and he has sleep overs for them when he has them.

I saw Jay's incredible love through the years. He sat and colored Easter eggs with them at Easter, he did every kind of craft, and play dough, and easy bake ovens. He swam with them in the summers and sledded with them in the winters. He juggled the needs of a boy and a girl. He would play little girl games with his daughter, yes, even Pretty-Pretty Princess, he looked ridiculous with his crown and earrings. He'd take them bowling and theme parks, Chucky Cheese and corn mazes, he read tons of stories, watched cartoons, and of course went to the park.

He has always brought them to church and taught them about God. His biggest concern has always been what was best for them, always. It was never a competition with him. If they wanted their mom on his time, they got their mom. He loves them truly, completely and unselfishly.

Jay received one last blow. After several years his ex-wife decided to move again. She took the kids out of school and went. Jay got a lawyer and fought it but when she convinced him the school, she was putting them in was better, so he dropped the case. He did not get to see them as often.

One good thing that happened was the court gave him a tax exemption. His IRS bill began shrinking instead of growing.

In my son's life he has been given big tests. He has faced disappointments and heart aches and loss. But he has faced them without becoming bitter and without giving up. He has passed his test. It was not over in one year or two, it lasted a long time.

With the kids gone Jay had time on his hands. He decided to try an online dating service. It sounds crazy to me, and I did not even know he did it, I only knew all of a sudden, he was dating someone. I hadn't met her, but she had a beautiful name, Laurielle.

He met her in October, a month after his kids had left for the summer. He liked her immediately. Their first date was the corn maze and their second was zip lining. They kept seeing each other. They both love to cook, and they would get together and cook.

His birthday is on December 6. For years his birthday had come and gone with little hoop-lah. He would get his usual gift from mom and dad, socks and underwear. Not this year, Laurielle celebrated his birthday with him. She gave him a present every hour, all day long. He loved it!

He had also brought home the home-made cake she made him and put it in my freezer. It had a layer of ice cream in it, and it was huge. I wanted a piece, but Jay was not home to ask. It was so big that I decided I could cut a piece and he would never notice, so I did. I never tasted anything so delicious in my life. I had to have another piece. I did and Jay forgave me and in fact he let me eat most of that cake, I was hooked on that cake, and we were all hooked on Laurielle.

Laurielle is as special as Jay. She is bright and peppy and fun. She is smart and beautiful. I was hoping she was going to stick around. But that was just the beginning. Jay was offered a new job as a car salesman. That was the break he had been waiting for. Jay had put himself through college with sales. He walked into a huge office of salesman and within the first month he was top seller. In fact, he so exceeded all the other salesmen that they wanted him to train the others. They called him "Sellin McClellan" He can sell! I had been hoping he would get a job in sales!

Jay's finances started turning around. Soon Jay was no longer driving an ancient junker, he was driving his dream car, or should I say truck, a Chevy Silverado. God was giving Jay his hearts desires.

And then one day he was goofing off in the office where he works being funny as always making everyone laugh, when a man who was producing a comedy at the community theatre saw him. He asked him to please come and try out for the play; he had a part he thought Jay would be perfect for. Jay went and tried out; they begged him to take the part. It was a three man play with one character being the funny man and that was Jay.

The play ran for three weeks and on opening night I had gall bladder surgery. I couldn't see the play until the next weekend, and I couldn't wait. My dad saw it first. He was amazed at Jay's performance. He told me, "You are not going to believe what your son is capable of!" He was right, the play was great! I had to go twice; I had to see it again. I have a collage framed on my office wall of newspaper clippings and pictures of Jay in his play. It was a special time I will never forget. It meant even more to me because I knew God was giving me my promise of total restoration. It was something Jay always wanted to do.

Just recently Jay and Laurielle were married. It was no ordinary wedding. It was beautiful; they were married in a castle. And Jay and Laurielle went on a real honeymoon trip to Florida. That is big stuff to me; vacations were not something we could afford, in fact that is a dream of mine to take a real vacation. To me that is the icing on the cake.

The icing on the cake for Jay is the wonderful relationship Kellan and Mikaila have with Laurielle. Now, they have a beautiful house, two dogs and sometimes four kids. {They have two foster children.} Jay's life has been restored, beyond what I could have imagined. It did not happen overnight, it took many years, but it happened.

The important key to this story is Jay's response to what he went through. Not that he was always perfect and did not struggle, he did. But for the love of his children, he faced the situation over and over and over and over and over again. He was misused taken advantage of and twisted like a pretzel. I know many men just leave and never see their children or rarely see their children, I don't blame them, they can't stand the pain, the anger, the frustration and they run.

Jay not only faced it, for the love of his children, he overcame it. I wish I could tell you that I did as well as he did, but I did not. The pain of having someone in control of my dear ones, my grandchildren, was a hindrance to me. I was afraid to let myself love them the way I did before. I was afraid of the pain. I am being restored also.

The Lord did pick Jay back up and cared for him and poured out His healing oil. God did it His way and in His time, but He did it the best way. He gently and lovingly picked up the broken pieces of Jay and his children's lives; He carefully and lovingly cared for his needs. He is the Good Samaritan and comes to us when everyone else passes us by.

Life will give us tests, hard, miserable, painful tests. We can face them bravely like Jay did knowing that it is God that sees our pain and loss and He is our rewarder and rescuer. And most of all, like the Good Samaritan, He will pick us up and restore us, personally.

Chapter Nineteen

Breaking Up the Prisons

The Spirit of the Lord is upon Me, because He has anointed Me to preach the gospel to the poor; He has sent me to heal the broken hearted, to proclaim liberty to the captives, And recovery of sight to the blind, To set at liberty those who are oppressed. Luke 4:18

Earlier in the book we talked about souls being shattered and held in prisons. I have seen these prisons on several occasions while praying but I did not understand them completely until I read Anna Mendez Farrell's book, Regions of Captivity.

Keep in mind these are real places in the spirit realm and they hold real captives. I have had some interesting experiences praying people out of some of these prisons. Although at first, I had no understanding of what I was seeing, I would just see a picture, as I prayed, and pray it through like I always do.

One time as we, my sister daughter and I, were praying we had quite an experience there. The last time my husband checked himself into rehab I felt God wanted me to call a prayer meeting before he came home. I knew God wanted to do something, but I had no idea what. So, I called together my prayer partners Carol and Joy to help me.

We set up a chair in the middle of the room and I sat in it, representing Jim. Then we all began to pray. Immediately the praying was intense, and the Holy Spirit began revealing things. We started singing, "There is power in the name of Jesus, to break every chain, to break every chain to break every chain."

We began breaking chains off of Jim. Joy saw the chains break off Jim except the ones on his right arm; they were from his past, so we kept praying. At this point Carol and Joy both saw Jim in a cave. And even though the cave had a demonic jailer, to our complete surprise the cave was not that bad. Carol saw that there were beautiful gemstones imbedded in the wall of the cave. She realized that Jim had spent his whole life in this cave, and these were the treasures of his salvation. They were in his cave because he could not leave there.

{I have always said my husband lives in an invisible cell because he has always had a corner of the house that he lived in, it was usually by the television. He eats, sleeps and stays there. We could visit him, but he didn't want us around most of the time. I never slept with my husband until after about twenty years of marriage I put a television in the bedroom and his cell moved to the bedroom. Now he has a cell mate, me. He tolerates me there, but he loves it if I leave him alone.]

As we prayed the chains came loose from the walls of the cave and the cave started to break up. Then as we prayed the walls began breaking up and releasing the gems imbedded in them. We were literally mining in the spirit through prayer.

Confirmation

Now, if you are reading this and thinking this is way out, I have had those thoughts myself many times as well and this time also. But God always seems give us confirmation and He did this time also. In fact, He amazed me. God had this thing planned way ahead of time.

A couple of weeks before this, I had gone with my grandson, David, who was eight years old to a rock shop. David is fascinated by rocks and gems and loves to study them. Of course, he wanted to buy them all, but they were way too expensive, so we bought him one thing and left.

A few days later I was shopping at garage sales, as I often do, and I found a rock mining kit that had never been opened. On the box it said there were fourteen rocks and gems in the box. I thought of how much they were at the rock shop and bought it for David, it was only two dollars. I thought I would give it to him for his birthday or Christmas or something and brought it home and threw it in the closet.

David and Jim have always been especially close, and David even looks like a little Jim. Well, it just so happened that David came with Joy the day we had prayer, his brother and sister were at their dad's house, and we only had David. So that we could have prayer in the living room uninterrupted, I put David in our bedroom and tried to think of something to keep him busy. The rock kit! I pulled it out of the closet and gave it to him and went out and we had the prayer time I just described.

As we were praying for the gems to be released from the walls from the cave, which took some time, in comes David. We hadn't seen him for a half hour or so as we were praying. He was so cute! He had on a little pair of goggles and was covered with dust. He had a small wooden chisel in his hand and his box containing gems imbedded in plaster of paris. He had chiseled out most of his gems but came out to ask how many he was supposed to find.

All of a sudden, the significance hit us. As we were in prayer mining out Jim's gems from the cave in the spirit realm, David was our little Jim, he came out of Jim's "cave" the bedroom carrying gems he had been mining. We couldn't believe the significance. It hit us so funny we actually stopped praying and just laughed for about five minutes straight.

{How do you do this stuff God?}

We prayed for several hours that day breaking up prisons and one thing we noticed was other family members were imprisoned in a series of cave adjoining each other. As we broke up Jim's cave it was doing damage to other caves and light was getting in. It was quite an experience. I wish I could tell you that Jim doesn't sit in his invisible cell anymore, but I can't, although he seemed to come out for a while. But Jim has had his longest sober period of his life. He got out of rehab almost two years ago and he is still sober.

Normally these caves are hideous places with horrible happenings from our past being relived over and over. Satan's goal is to imprison our souls and render us ineffective in our lives. He also wants to shatter our souls and torment us. He wants to keep us trapped and broken our entire lives. He is behind the things that destroy us things like abuse, hatred, violence, sickness, divorce perversion, rape and sin, and many more.

God has a plan for our lives, a good plan which we were created to do. Satan also has a plan for us, a plan to destroy us and use us to destroy others and directly oppose God. And if Satan is successful in his plan, he claims a soul at death and torments it endlessly. He starts by breaking our hearts.

The day God led us to pray for Jim, and as we were breaking up the caves, it was doing damage to other caves. At one point as we were praying Joy saw a soul that shot right up out of hell, from a damaged cage. We wondered what that could mean. We didn't have to wait long.

The next week Joy received a call from her ex-husband, Donald. He had once served the Lord but now he wouldn't even discuss it. I had tried to talk to him about the Lord and he replied, "I don't believe in that anymore." He was dating a young girl named Amy whom we did not know much about.

Joy drove up to my house and ran out of her car to my door. I wondered what the matter could possibly be. "Mom" she cried, "Donald is on his way here with Amy, he just called he is hysterical. He says she is manifesting a demon!"

Before she even finished telling me Donald's car came racing around the corner and screeched into my driveway. The door popped open, and Donald jumped out screaming, "Help her! Please help her!! She needs prayer!!"

Amy was in the front seat of the car writhing and her eyes were rolled back in her head. She looked sort of like she was having a grand mall seizure. Donald yelled something about a satanic ritual she had been through.

Joy and I looked at each other wondering what in the world to do. I said to Joy, "Let's just get her saved and let Jesus help her."

That was the plan, so we set to work. We got her out of the car onto the porch. She was still writhing, and her eyes were still rolled back, but when we asked her if she wanted to ask Jesus into her heart, she nodded her head, yes.

We prayed with her but there was no change. I felt the Lord whisper to take her in the back yard and baptize her in the pool, but I did not get the chance to tell Joy because Donald was screaming so much that he was scaring the three little kids. I took him in the house and tried to calm him down. I reminded him that he knew the Lord and he settled down some.

By this time the kids had all jumped in the pool. Donald and I went back on the porch and by this time Amy was praying in tongues, but her appearance hadn't changed, she was still writhing. Joy said what I was thinking, "We are supposed to baptize her."

I don't even remember getting to the pool, but we got there quick because of the shape she was in. She was writhing in the pool as I said; "I baptize you in the name of the Father and the Son and the Holy Spirit"

She went down into the water and then came up. As she wiped the water from her face and opened her eyes a big smile came to her face. It was the first time we saw her eyes. Her face was glowing, she threw her head back and began laughing for joy!

She was our soul that shot up out of hell!

The next Sunday both she and Donald were in church. Amy was still glowing.

The spirit world is the real world. Our world is affected by it. Prayer is powerful and not to be taken lightly. We had no idea what was going to happen when we met to pray or what the result would be. The Holy Spirit was the mastermind, we just followed His leading.

One thing I gained new respect for through all of this was baptism. I literally felt the power of God hit her as we brought her up out of the water. There is something wonderful that happens through baptism, even in a backyard swimming pool!

A work of Jesus on earth which is now the work of His body, us, the believers, is to set captives free. We may not always see a jail and face a demonic guard. We may be led by the Holy Spirit in other ways. Sometimes a word of truth spoken in love sets others free, never underestimate the power of love. And of course, as always prayer; remember what the Bible says the effectual, fervent prayer of the righteous avails much.

Chapter Twenty

Healed on Earth or In Heaven
Part 1

And God will wipe away every tear from their eyes; there shall be no more death, nor sorrow, nor crying. There shall be no more pain, for the former things have passed away.
Revelation 21:4

There are those who are so broken that they will never be repaired in this lifetime. I found that out one time during a conversation with the Lord in prayer.

I was praying for someone; we'll call her Sally. Sally was a single mother to two little girls. She was dating and soon to be married to an awful man. He had some kind of an emotional hold on her and no matter what I said to her about him she would not listen. I asked the Lord if I was overreacting and if maybe things would be okay.

He told me, "No, if Sally marries this man, the damage to Sally's daughters will be so great that I will not be able to heal them during their life on earth. I will heal them in heaven but on earth they will never be healed."

I hadn't known before that conversation with the Lord that some people become so damaged through abuse that they cannot be healed on earth. I thought God could fix all of us on earth. I was counting on that for myself, and I wanted it done quickly.

Sally's story ends happily, although for a time I thought things would go the other way. I got nowhere talking to Sally. Several weeks later as I still struggled with the situation in prayer an anger rose up in me and I bound the devil. I told him he could not destroy Sally's girls, or Sally and I bound him in Jesus name. The next day Sally's fiancé left and never returned. He soon married someone else.

My point is that even if someone is so broken, they cannot be healed, God will not reject them. He still wants them, and He has planned their deliverance for when they come home to Him in heaven. He doesn't discard hopelessly wounded souls. If you are too broken to be healed, God still wants you. He has a special day planned for you, a day He is anticipating even more than you are. The day He will make you whole.

We are going to be healed whether it is on earth or it is in heaven, but we will be healed. Jesus told us He came to give us life and that more abundantly. Have you ever wondered if you will ever see that fulfilled? I have.

Some people live and die and never seem to see their dreams fulfilled. And with some people it is even worse than that they live their whole lives broken, they seem broken beyond repair. They live their lives alone and forgotten. They never seem to make it. They are the cast offs of society.

I can write this book because that is me, that is me and my husband, we are with you in that category. There is hope.

A Healing River

One of my favorite books that I have read over and over countless times through the years is called, *Intra Muros*. The book is written by a woman named Rebecca Springer. The book was written in 1898 and has been a classic inspiration ever since. Rebecca had poor health most of her life and at one point was unconscious for days. While unconscious she experienced heaven, not just for days but for a period of years. She literally had a life in heaven. It is one of those unexplainable things and she does not try to explain but she says she simply tells the story as she experienced it.

Her story starts as she is laying very ill in her bed and her brother in law, Frank who had died several years before comes and lifts her up and carries her to heaven. As he brings her into Paradise, he sets her down gently in a beautiful spot surrounded by flowers near a river.

This river is a healing river. It is of course the River of Life. It is essential for those entering heaven to begin in the river, which is exactly what Rebecca does. After she goes in the River a change takes place.

Thus encouraged, I, too, stepped into the gently flowing River. To my great surprise I found the water, in both temperature and density, almost identical to the air. Deeper and deeper grew the stream as we passed on, until I felt the soft sweet ripples playing about my throat. As I stopped Frank said, "A little farther still."

"It will be over my head," I reasoned.

"Well, and what then?'

"I cannot breathe under water—I will suffocate."

An amused twinkle came to his eyes, though he said soberly enough, "We do not do those things here."

I realized the absurdity of my position and with a happy laugh said, "All right." Then I plunged headlong into the bright water, which soon bubbled and rippled several feet above my head. To my surprise and delight, I found I could breathe, laugh, talk, see and, hear as naturally under the water as above

"What marvelous water! What marvelous air!" I said to Frank, as we again stepped upon the flowery field. "Are all rivers here like this one?'

"Not exactly the same but similar," he replied.

We walked on a few steps, and then I turned and looked back at the shining river flowing on tranquilly. "Frank, what has this water done for me? I feel as though I could fly."

He looked at me with earnest, tender eyes, as he answered gently, "It has washed away the last of the earth life and prepared you for the new life upon which you have entered."

"It is divine," I whispered.

"Yes, it is divine," he said.

Frank's job was to get Rebecca in the river. She needed healing. She was fearful and worried. That washed away in the river.

We all will be healed in heaven. We will be healed physically, spiritually and emotionally. Our broken hearts and wounded souls will be healed, and we will become the person God created us to be. Rebecca underwent healing in the River of Life.

Later in the book Rebecca is called upon to help with a man who entered heaven but refused to go in the river. Everyone has special duties in heaven and Rebecca's father would help newly arrived souls. On this day he calls on Rebecca for help.

"I am faced with the most difficult problem I have yet to deal with in this work. It is how to enlighten and help a man who suddenly plunged from an apparently honorable life into the very depths of crime. I have never been able to get him to accompany me to the river, where these earthly cobwebs would be swept from his poor brain. His excuse is always that God's mercy is so great in allowing him inside heaven's gates at all, that he is content to remain always in its lowest scale of enjoyment and life. No argument or teaching thus far has helped him alter his decision.

"He was led astray by infatuation for a strange woman and killed his aged mother in order to secure her jewels for this wretched creature. He was executed for the crime, of which at the end he sincerely repented, but he left life with all the horror of the deed clinging to his soul."

I find this story absolutely fascinating. First of all, because it shows the grace of God is so amazing that even a man who murders his own mother can find forgiveness. Secondly, is that now that he is in heaven, they have the job of healing his soul. The Lord entrusts this work to His servants and Rebecca and her father are lovingly and gently handling the matter. They are trying to decide what to do.

Rebecca asks her father, "Has he seen the Master?"

"No, he begs not to see Him. He is very repentant and grateful to be saved from the wrath he feels was his just punishment. Though he is conscious that his sin is forgiven, he does not feel that he can ever stand in the presence of the Holy One. And here, as on earth, each must be willing to receive Him."

Rebecca decides to bring the man's mother to him.

135

They had not brought her sooner because they had hoped the reunion between this man and his mother would be after her son had been better prepared. Rebecca goes to the mother and explains the situation to her. The mother eagerly comes with Rebecca.

We found the young man seated beneath one of the flower laden trees, intently studying a book my father had left with him. There was a peaceful look on his pale face, but it was rather the look of patient resignation than overwhelming joy. His mother approached him alone. My father and I remained in the background. After a while, he glanced up and saw his mother standing near him. A startled look came into his face, and he rose to his feet. She extended her arms toward him and cried out pathetically, "John, my dear boy, come home to me—I need you!" That was all.

With a low cry he knelt at her feet and clasped her knees, sobbing, "Mother! Mother!"

My father had explained to the mother that the first thing to be accomplished was to get her son to the river. We now heard her say caressingly. "Come, John, my boy, take the first step upward, for your mother's sake, that in time I may have the joy of seeing you in our home. Come, John, with mother."

She gently drew him, and to our great joy we saw him rise and go with her. The steps led them to the river. They walked hand in hand, and as far as we could see them, she seemed to be soothing and comforting him.

"There will be no further trouble now," said my father. "When they return, he will see with clearer vision." And so, it was.

A mother murdered by her own son, the son,

horrified by his own actions; these things have to be dealt with and healed for all time. This marvelous River of Life was essential. The River of Life proceeds from God. It flows from Him. The River of Life is love, God's love. It has the power to heal us.

You will have your day in this River. This is a healing place where the heaviness of this world is washed out of us, and we are restored.

Neville Johnson, a wonderful man of God, who spends much time in heaven, tells of seeing people come to this River. He has also said in his sermons a time of great healing is coming to earth and this river is coming to earth for this time. Many on earth will receive healing, in this way. We are living in great times. The River of Life is coming to earth. But whether on earth or in heaven we will all come to this River.

Our Greatest Need

God has lovingly planned our healing and it brings Him great joy to heal us. For some their healing will take place when they see Him, like my husband Jim. Jim's greatest need is for a father, and Jim's final healing will not be until he stands before the Father and the greatest need is met. Jim has changed dramatically since we have been married but his biggest need has not been met. He is still very wounded, and he won't be totally healed until his greatest need for a father is met. That day will come.

God used Jim, in my life, to meet my greatest need. In my heart I had rejected living. There was a form of me still going on and going through my everyday life, but I wasn't really living. I had no desire to be here. I put forth no effort. I refused to try. I was dead inside. I wasn't conscious of this decision because I had made in the womb, but it had affected my life ever since.

God put Jim in my path to awaken me. In an instant everything changed for me. Somehow in a matter of seconds I wanted something. I wanted something with all my being.

I told how Jim managed to touch the real person in me in my book about our marriage, *The Impossible Marriage.* That one moment took place in the back seat of my parent's car. My parents had picked up Jim from Detroit and were bringing him home. They had a prison ministry and had been writing to Jim while he was in prison. Once he got out, he was not doing well, and they had driven to get him and were going to try and help him.

I was sitting in the back seat with Jim. I was clutching my doll, Snooks. Even though I was seventeen I still held my doll. I slept with her every night. She was the first thing I would pick up when I got home from school. She was well worn from my years of holding her. Most of the paint on her rubbery face had faded away. But I didn't care, to me she was beautiful. My doll was the most important thing in the world to me. I would hold her and stare at her face for hours. She was real to me; I could not be without her.

I was nervous being in the back seat with Jim and I was sitting as far away from him as I could. I did not want to talk to him. I was pressed up against the door and facing out the window, clutching Snooks.

Jim asked me if he could see my doll. Compliantly, as always, I handed Jim Snooks, and watched him, wondering. He handled her carefully and set her on his lap and just looked at her, like I always did. Then he kissed her.

In the twinkling of an eye my world changed, the moment before he was nobody, now he was the most important person in the world to me. All of a sudden, I wanted something, he was all I wanted. It was like the whole world was black and white and he was Technicolor. He was warm and the world was cold. I wanted to be with him, forever. Minutes passed like seconds when I was near him. I never wanted to leave.

I had a reason to live now, because I wanted something. Something that was impossible because Jim was not able to function outside of prison, it was all he knew, and he was soon locked up again.

Suddenly, I had to put forth effort. I had to pull together the little bit of a person there was inside me and try with everything I had.

There was really no hope for us. He was a mess; I was a mess, which equaled one big mess. Except we were on holy ground, God had a plan in this, and His grace was with us. I had to walk this invisible line with God. It took all my effort. It took faith, it took obedience. It took everything I could muster. And suddenly I had the will, because I wanted something.

That was thirty-nine years ago. I'm still being stretched past my endurance. But for thirty-nine years now God has successfully gotten me to move forward. He has gotten me to live, to move forward, and to use everything within me. It has been incredibly hard, but I am still moving forward. My marriage has met the biggest need for healing in me, it caused me to live.

Unmet Desires

God is not just going to meet our greatest need; he is going to meet the desires of our heart that were never fulfilled on earth. This too, is part of your healing.

Kat Kerr is a woman whom God has taken to heaven multiple times. In her many trips to heaven, she has learned how God meets unfulfilled desires. She has given many people comfort that have lost loved ones. She has seen them in heaven, and she describes to their families what she sees. She brings back hope from the other side. And one of the greatest things she has discovered, is God doesn't just heal us in heaven, He meets every unfulfilled desire.

In Kat's first book, *Revealing Heaven, an Eyewitness Account,* she tells the story of John. John had been married to Vickie a woman who worked in the church office. The Lord spoke to Kat on a Valentine's Day and told her to bring roses to Vickie from John. He told her also to tell Vickie that John loves her and misses her very much. Then, suddenly the heavens opened, and Kat saw John in heaven. She saw John playing golf with Jesus!

Kat was astounded to find out that there is golf in heaven. It was the most beautiful golf course she had ever seen and while she stood there staring, the Lord explained to her that this was John's backyard in heaven! She was shown his front yards also. It was huge and it was beautiful. In the front of his house he had a very royal looking deck overlooking a crystal sea and people would arrive by boat to come and play golf with John at his large spacious beautiful home, with complete 18-hole golf course!

I am going to quote from the book, the response she received from Vickie when Kat told her what she had seen.

"For the first few minutes after you told me about the vision you had of my husband, John {or Johnny as I called him} I meditated on it. I thought to myself, if you had told me you saw him playing pool or bowling it would have been an instant recognition of him since he

played both well. Then I realized by the Spirit that he had always wanted to play golf. In his latter years, he always watched the golf tournaments on television, read articles about it and even got a part time job with a golf supply company. Johnny had become very knowledgeable about the game. He said, "One of these days I am going to take golf lessons," but financially we couldn't afford it and therefore never realized that dream before he died. I cried after you shared with me about Heaven, because I realized Johnny had been given the desire of his heart. He not only was playing golf, but even had his own golf course. How wonderful God is to allow me to know about the gifts he gave Johnny and about the beautiful home he now lives in."

We have an existence ahead of us that we can't imagine at this time. We are not only going to be healed, we are going to be fulfilled and we are going to be doing things that we were created for, ruling and reigning with Christ. The healing we need will come, if not on earth it will happen in heaven.

Chapter Twenty-One

Healed on Earth or Healed in Heaven   Part Two

For you did not receive the spirit of bondage again to fear, but you received the Spirit of adoption by whom we cry out, "Abba Father." The spirit Himself bears witness that we are children of God. Romans 8:15-16

I want to take a deeper look at this topic, being healed on earth or being healed in heaven.

For years I prayed for a father figure for my husband. Remember I talked about Jim's greatest need. I knew it would change him. Jim did not know his real father. We had looked for him from time to time, but without success.

Jim had a fantasy about him, that he was rich, that he was a very great man, someone Jim could be very proud of. Jim had dreamed of this his whole life; he'd hoped his father would come into his life and change everything.

The day came when we actually found Jim's dad. The

social security office forwarded him our phone number and he called us. He was not what Jim had hoped for. He was a homeless man. He was an alcoholic and he was mentally ill. He got a on a bus and came to us with everything he owned, in a suitcase. I soon realized I could not have this man in our house near my two young daughters it was not safe. I made him leave. Jim found him a very inexpensive trailer for him to live in.

The truth was too much for Jim to handle. I lost Jim for a while. Jim had been doing fair for about a year. He had a good job at a supermarket near our house. He was training as a meat cutter. He had a year of training at entry pay and then when his training was complete his wage would double, and he would get benefits. I had a job I was hoping to be able to quit soon. I had been working every night delivering newspapers. My job was seven days a week and I was tired I wanted to sleep at night again and I was looking forward to his soon good paying job. His year of training was just about up when his dad arrived.

Jim could not handle his shattered dream of a father. Jim fell apart. He began drinking heavily. Jim's dad only made things worse; he wanted Jim to drink so he could keep him near him, he was lonely.

Jim lost his job just weeks before his promotion. It was awful. I did not even see him for days at a time. The shock of all of this took a toll on me also. My world had caved in again just when I thought everything was going to get better. It was so hard on me I couldn't even think straight.

I remember waking up one night at about one thirty a.m., to go to work. I went out to get in the car and in the dim streetlight, I could make out that there was a man lying in the middle of the street.

I gasped. A car could hit him and kill him! I hadn't seen Jim in days, and I wondered if it was him. Shaking in terror I ran to the man and rolled him over. I looked in his face and tried to see if it was Jim. Even though I was looking at the man's face I could not tell if it was Jim or not. I was near to being in shock and I could not discern what I was seeing. I ran and woke up my son. He was about fourteen at the time. Jamie had the same problem. He thought it was Jim's dad and shook the man saying, "Grampa, grampa!"

The man aroused, confused, and looked at us and we looked at him. We realized he was a stranger and Jamie helped him to his feet and the man staggered down the street.

The world seemed crazy. I wondered where Jim was. I hoped he was safe.

Eventually Jim was able to get himself checked into a mental health and addictions hospital and he was gone for four months. He managed to pull himself back together somewhat.

I continued to pray for a father for Jim, someone who would mentor him. One day, years later, God answered me. He said in His incredible voice, "I am Jim's Father."

God was revealing something to me; this need was not going to be met for Jim on earth. Jim's greatest need would be met, but not on earth. It was going to be met in a greater way, greater than I could possibly imagine.

Jim has another problem, also. Jim is terrified to die. Nothing I say to him seems to give him any relief. He thinks he is too bad, and he is not going to make it to heaven. He has had this fear ever since I have known him.

I say to Jim, "What are trusting for your salvation, your righteousness or Jesus righteousness?"

It doesn't seem to help. Or I have tried saying to him,

"If God wanted you in hell why would he send Jesus to die on the cross for your sins?"

I can't get through to him. I have given up.

As hopeless as Jim feels, he has never given up serving the Lord. He keeps trying to serve the Lord hoping he will make it, just as he has done since he gave his life to the Lord back in 1969. He just keeps trying.

God gave me a vision of Jim in heaven. I have told this to Jim also, but even this won't get through his thick head. I have said, "Jim, I saw you in heaven in a vision! You are going to make it!"

I can't get through to him; he gets that worried look on his face, and says, "I hope so."

The vision was so awesome, that it has changed my life, and makes me more in awe of our wonderful God. God was showing me the answer to my prayer.

I saw Jim in heaven, standing next to Jesus. Jesus had told Jim that He was going to present him to the Father. Jim was standing before the throne of God, head down, he dared not look up. He had that same look on his face I had seen a thousand times. Shame, he did not feel worthy and he dare not look up. But the look on the Lord's face was one of great joy as He stood next to Jim. Because He knew what was coming. Finally, with the help of the Lord Jesus, Jim looked up.

Jim's desire for a father, which he had since a small child, that greatest need within him, which caused him to a dream of a rich and powerful father, this time was met beyond his wildest dreams. As Jim lifted his eyes to the blinding light of the Father, he saw the greatest love, the greatest acceptance, from his Father, the God of the Universe. Every bit of shame and pain and fear melted as Jim was welcomed, into the Fathers heart, Jim disappeared into the brightness as the Father embraced him and drew Jim into His very being. I could not see Jim anymore.

I understood that it pleased the Father to wait for this moment to heal Jim. It was the perfect time for his healing because Jim's need for the Father resulted into a bond with God that was closer than most will ever know. I saw that from that moment on Jim would never be far from the Father. He did not want to leave Him, and that pleased God also.

I got to see the change in Jim. He was different. It was him but he was changed. I talked to him, and he was so at peace and so fulfilled. He looked good too. His expression, Jim has always got a worried expression, but not anymore, he was radiant.

He wore his hair differently also. Jim has naturally curly hair which he always flattens but his hair was a little longer and curly. Jim just looked so good. But the biggest change was that I could tell he was totally fulfilled, and the fulfillment was his relationship with the Father.

I felt a little in awe of his close position with God.

I started realizing something about God. He is allowing Jim's pain to continue until this day for a reason.

The wheels were turning in my head. I remembered that a few weeks ago Jim started complaining, again, that he was so afraid to die. Joy and I started to pray for him. I was asking God to give Jim a sign somehow that he would make it to heaven. But I felt like God said, "No."

I kept praying and I was feeling that Jim's suffering was somehow precious to God. Then Joy said it. She said, "The fact that dad puts forth such effort even though he doubts his salvation is precious to God."

That started some more wheels turning in my head. I started wondering about myself. I still feel like such a mess.

146

Oh Yes, I have come such a long way, but I still have some huge issues. One of my big issues is my fear of someone with alcohol on their breath. {usually Jim] It is not a normal fear. It is terror and I shut down.

So, here I am with this terrible fear, which God has never healed in me, and I am married to an alcoholic! I face this fear over and over and over.

In fact, I had a real problem when God told me to write my story, *The Impossible Marriage*. I thought I should not be such a mess. God should heal me first, or even better Jim should never, ever drink again! When my book did not get off too much of a start, I thought maybe God is waiting to fix me better. How can such a mess tell others about marriage?

But the wheels have been turning in my head. Maybe God is not going to heal me of this fear, now. Could it be that, because I am married to an alcoholic, and I have a fear of alcohol, is the reason I can write a book about marriage? The fact that the hardest thing for me to face is what I have had to face in my marriage, and I have faced it, terrified but I have faced it, and I came to the place where I decided if Jim never quit drinking, I was not going anywhere, I was staying with him no matter what, even though it meant continuing to have to face that fear. Was this the reason I could speak to marriages?

But that is not all I am having trouble with. I still have problems with my fear of living. Even though I don't live in constant fear of people anymore, I still have tenderness. I often have to cry out to God on the way to work because I feel afraid. I need Him to help me face the world each day. He has healed me enough to do it, but I still feel a bit vulnerable.

Is that there for a reason? Do I still need to have pain

so I can write to the hurting? Maybe the complete healing I am waiting for will not take place in this life. I thought about Paul again also. God kept that question there, "Did Paul make it to Heaven?"

He told me He wanted me tender to the broken hearted. I started to realize something else; God is impressed with us, hurting people, when we keep going on, even though we are weak and broken, for the love of Him, for the love of our mates, for the love of our children, for the love of others. We won't quit even though we feel like quitting. This is holy ground to God.

This may be what He is looking for. Those of us who keep marching through the darkness of this world, toward Him, against all odds, our weaknesses don't stop us, our fears don't stop us, and adversities don't stop us.

Maybe He hasn't healed us completely for a reason, because we are called to a high calling in Him, a calling of love, and we are proving ourselves worthy.

Oh, yes, we will be healed, we will be completely whole, but it may take just a little bit longer, but if it does, that is okay. If not on earth, it will be in heaven.

Chapter Twenty-Two

Finally

{Now this, "He ascended" what does it mean but that He also first descended into the lower parts of the earth? He who descended is also the One who ascended far above all the heavens, that He might fill all things.] Ephesians 4:9-10

My Dear brokenhearted brothers and sisters in Christ,

Your situation may look bleak and hopeless. You may feel worthless, or that you have fallen through the cracks. You may be carrying around a feeling of grief like a heavy weight. Or you may be tired of your situation that never seems to end.

I want to leave you with one last word of hope. I want to pull back the dark and heavy curtain that is blocking your view, and give you a glimmer of the bright, shining, sunlight that is on the other side. Your brokenness qualifies you for great beauty. You have a value that you will never be able to understand in this lifetime. You are standing on holy ground. God is nearer to you now than you can possibly realize. You are His first priority. His attention is on you. There is hope for you, great hope.

I am thinking of Betsy ten Boom's last words whispered as she lay dying in a concentration camp. She said, **"There is no pit so deep that He is not deeper still."**

There truly is no pit that His love does not go deeper still. Jesus descended to the lowest pit, and He now fills all in all.

Betsy lived in one of the most horrible times in earth, during World War 2, in one of the most horrible places on earth, a concentration camp. Evil seemed to reign over good. People became as depraved as demons in their sadistic treatment of other human beings. In the midst of all that suffering, horror, and evil was Betsy's finest hour.

How can that be?

In the deepest darkness, Betsy shone brightly. She proved her love, not only for other human beings, she proved her love for God.

She was an aging spinster; she had lived a quiet life. She wasn't Jewish; she did not have to share their fate. She could have been sympathetic but stay uninvolved. But not only did she choose to help the Jewish people, when she was caught and thrown into a concentration camp where she was starved and literally worked to death, she died with no hatred for anyone.

Betsy left us a testimony. **"There is no pit so deep that He does not go deeper still."**

The farther down, the deeper the love, the greater the price, the greater the grace. This may look like your bleakest moment, but I want you to see it differently. In fact, I want you to see life differently.

There is a work being done in your heart, an important work. Jesus faced a cross and hell. Betsy faced a concentration camp. What are you facing?

I often feel like I am standing in front of a heavy door,

it is dark and terrible and full of fear. The pain and foreboding of the future are terrifying, because I do not know what is ahead. Do you ever feel like that too?

But we do know, Who is ahead, and He's also behind and beside us. He is the God who was and is and is to come. He is timeless and eternal, and He is also waiting behind that door. So, all we can do is take one step at a time and face what is behind that door, with Him. We may not see Him, or we may not feel Him, but He is there.

We may face pain, but that is okay, because facing our pain brings healing. Go ahead and face the pain. We may shed tears, but that is okay because remember tears produce joy and blessing. Every one of those tears are being kept and stored in a bottle. We may face trials and heart aches and suffering; we are gaining authority. We may feel alone but all of heaven is watching us, hoping for us and rooting for us. We may feel insignificant, but you are a priority, we are of the utmost importance. It may seem like our hearts are breaking more, but they are not, they are being healed. But our hearts must remain tender so that our hearts will be alert and attentive to God and others.

Pain is Temporary

I was watching a Christian television show yesterday, *Its Supernatural,* with Sid Roth, and something stood out to me, probably because I was working on this book. Sid had two other ministers with him on the show, and one of them was a man named Keith, Keith kept mentioning his heart was broken, and then tears would come to his eyes. I kept wondering what happened to him. After he said it about the third time, Sid said to the audience that Keith just lost his wife.

Then Keith explained he had been happily married for 45 years. He had met his wife when he was sixteen years old in high school, and his wife died just before Christmas. There was pain in Keith's face as he spoke, and the tears started. He truly was broken hearted; it was written on his face. He seemed to be coping with the constant help of Christian friends, of whom he was very grateful for.

Then he said that he recently had been having one of his worst days. He was in the car with his son, who was driving, when his cell phone rang. Keith hadn't been answering his phone or taking calls, but he felt prompted to answer. He was surprised to find out the call was from Jesse Duplantis. {Jesse is a wonderful minister who happened to have a visit to heaven in 1988 and wrote a great book about it.}

Jesse told Keith he had been praying for him and the Lord told him to call him and tell him something. He told Keith, "One day to the Lord is as a thousand years and a thousand years as a day." Then he added, "If you live to be a hundred years old and then get to heaven your wife Cheryl will say to you, 'Keith, we have only been apart twenty minutes.'"

As Keith told this, Sid interjected, "Keith, why are you getting so upset for over twenty minutes?"

For the first time Keith smiled and then laughed, it seemed to bring him comfort.

Keith is now in a hard time of mourning, but the real message his friends are reminding him of is this; that for the Christian, all pain is only temporary. It is only for the moment, but it will soon pass away. Not only will the pain pass, God will totally restore and totally fulfill every person that comes to Him. He is love, remember? He also desires for that day to come, even more than you do.

The Father feels every emotion that you feel and more. I totally get this. It is harder for me to see my children in pain than to go through pain myself. And their joy is my joy. I have often prayed, "If I have any reward coming in this life, Lord, please give it to my children and my grandchildren." If we love our children this much, how much more does God love us?

Pain is only temporary and the joy, that will come, it far outweighs the pain. This is so because of the great love our God and Father has for us.

"I Want to Feel Better Now!"

I have been having a hard time lately. The problem is that nothing is really wrong, but somehow, I have emotionally fallen off a cliff and I am feeling pain and grief. It kind of took me by surprise, but even so it overpowered me. I had been looking forward to my son's wedding for months. Jay had met Laurielle over two years before, and from the moment I met this wonderful girl, I had been hoping this day would come. {You know this I wrote about it in another chapter.}

When they set the date and made plans, I requested 5 days off from work so I would even have an extra two days off afterwards. They got married in March, but January and February were hard months for me. I usually have every other weekend off, but I had to work them. I kept telling myself, "It is okay, I need the money for wedding stuff, and I have five whole days off in March, for Jay and Laurielle's wedding." I trudged through by looking forward to the wedding.

The time finally came. I was packed several days

ahead of time in anticipation. His wedding was in a darling little town a little more than an hour away. We had the rehearsal on Friday afternoon and the wedding on Saturday afternoon. Jim and I had booked a hotel to stay in Friday and Saturday night, months before; I had spent hours online picking the place. Everything seemed perfect. And did I mention Jay and Laurielle were getting married in a castle?

It was even better than I could have imagined. Jay happened to get the same hotel and I had my two grandchildren there to swim with me. Swimming is my favorite thing to do; and I can't remember the last time I got to swim in an indoor pool, and swimming with my grandchildren was better yet. The pool was even open twenty-four hours. I swam six times in two days; both days I got up at the crack of dawn and had the pool all to myself.

Everything was fun, on Friday before I left my daughter Lonna cut and styled my hair and gave me a new pair of earrings. I was all dolled up for the rehearsal dinner, which was fun. Then on Saturday before the wedding both daughters came early and both of them did my hair and makeup for the wedding {fun, fun, fun}. I had a beautiful new dress and shoes to wear that they bought me.

The wedding was a dream. It was so beautiful. The bride was stunning; I think she was the prettiest bride ever. Jay was so handsome, and Jim, my husband, was also in a tux and so was my grandson Kellan. My granddaughter Mikaila looked cuter than I had ever seen her, she was the junior bridesmaid. She had spent the morning with her new stepmom at the beauty parlor, and she had a long flowing gown to match the bridesmaids. I was so happy I cried.

Sunday morning more swimming and then a brunch given by the bride's mother, and we watched the bride and groom open their presents. Then Jim and I got in the car and started driving home.

That is when it hit me.

Pain!

My heart felt like there was a knife stuck in it. It was over and I had to go back to my life. NOOOOOOO!!!!!

On a scale of one to ten this was about an eight and a half, this was bad. I had suffered from depression before; this wasn't totally new. The first time was post-partum depression after my second child was born. It was horrible, but I made up my mind I would get through it. When my emotions kept telling me life wasn't worth living, I rejected it and kept telling myself, "These feelings aren't real, they will pass," and after a couple of weeks they did. I also would go through depression after my many surgeries; I realized it was from the pain meds. It was especially bad after the kidney's stones; I had spent a couple of days on a morphine pump, and the blues afterwards were terrible.

I hate being hit by depression, and here it was again, it snuck up and clobbered me after my son's wedding. I walked around with a lead weight in my chest and choking back tears.

It so surprised me I had to stop and ask myself why I was feeling this way. I realized I felt trapped with no way out. I need to work because I need the money, but I can't make enough money and I am tired of working!!!!!Looking forward to the wedding kept my focus ahead, now it was over.

"God, I don't want to go through pain! I want to feel better now!"

In my mind, my life ahead was drudgery, endless drudgery.

"Help me God, it seems like my life is over."

It seems like every time I write a book I go through

another test. I guess I am going through the broken heart test with you. So, I am going to face it and remember, these feelings will pass. I may feel like I am wandering around in the dark, but God can see what is ahead of me. He wants me to trust Him. Let's trust Him together. Let's believe that this is all going to work for good. Let's keep going forward and let's face our pain.

And finally, I want to remember Paul, once again. In this life he never overcame the pain, he died broken. But I am hoping with all my heart he is now healed.

Will you do something for Paul? Will you reach out to those who are like him and remember him? Will you stay tender to those who are hurting also, and give them a word of hope?

God loves them.

They are on God's priority list

All pain is temporary

God will restore them

God will not waste their suffering, they will be strong in their broken places

They are gaining authority

Jesus inside them will be their normal, though the outside is in turmoil, their inside can know peace.

Tears can be a special prayer and they produce fruit.

We all have something to look forward to. We have a future and a hope. We have a God that has good things planned for us. If we are beaten up at this time, we know He is coming to restore us. He is our Good Samaritan.

And please remember, God is not judging your life like others do. Was everything stacked against you? Have you fallen through the cracks of life? When you look at your life is all that you see brokenness?

That does not mean you are on the bottom of the

pecking order. It means you have potential for greater authority.

Remember the Japanese art we talked about? The beautiful pieces were the ones with more breaks; they were filled with more gold. The broken places in your life are the places God can use. He will fill them with Himself. They will be your strongest places.

If you feel like your life is over let me remind you; you are an eternal being, created in the image of God, Himself. You will still be here in eons to come, with Him, happy restored and whole, fulfilling your purpose and totally fulfilled, beyond your imagination!

Are you beginning to see that light I promised you yet? Do you see that if all you can do is just pull yourself up and face your fears one more time that you are doing something greater than you can possibly ever imagine? It is something. It is something big and God will use just that. Keep going. There is destiny ahead of you. You are determining your eternal position now. Every time you pull yourself up again you move up and up and up. You are getting stronger.

There was a point I thought my life had been wasted. I gave it to God, but I thought He had wasted it. My whole life had been spent in tears crossing a desert and yet the end was still not in sight. But then I turned around and looked, I found myself in a garden, planted by my own tears. My life had not been wasted after all; it was beautiful.

And I can't help but keep thinking about Jesus. He followed the Father perfectly. He never wavered for a moment. Yet it led Him to a cross and torture and death and then hell. The lowest hell and the lowest pit there is. He looked like a failure, to everyone who followed Him and especially to His enemies. They were delighted at His fall.

For the first time In Jesus existence, He was separated from the Father.

And then Satan taunted and tormented Him and reminded Him of His failure over and over. The heart of Jesus was broken and shattered to a million pieces. In hell Jesus had to remember His identity in the Father. He did that by looking within Himself and He did that by remembering scripture. He held onto truth.

But from this lowest place Jesus overcame and He has filled all things. Now He holds the highest place. Now there is no place His love can't reach you. He is the King of Kings and the Lord of Lords and at His name every knee will bow, not only in heaven and earth but under the earth. He is victorious.

Is Satan reminding you of your failure, over and over? Is he tormenting you?

Your identity is in Christ. You are complete in Him. That is truth that you can hold onto through anything.

Betsy ten Boom did. She held onto truth in the midst of hell. She never became like those around her, full of hate because she held onto love. And she whispered that truth as she died. I think I will end the book with her words. Words to give you hope.

"There is no pit so deep, that He is not deeper still."

Epilogue

If you have somehow read this book and you have not yet come to Jesus, this is your invitation now. Would you like to give your broken heart to Jesus? He will fill it with His love. I gave my heart to the Lord when I was fourteen years old. I did not pray a prayer I hollered, "I want God!" That was all it took. Just tell Him you want Him. It was His love that drew me to Him. I never felt such love in my life. If you truly want to be loved, just as you are, then you want Jesus too. Let's tell Him; Lord, I need you and I want you. Please forgive my sins and come into my heart. I will live for You, Amen.

Note to the reader,

I believe with all my heart, that because of Missy's influence on Paul, Paul's heart was stirred. I believe a short window opened in which Paul's heart was receptive to the Spirit of God. God in His incredible love for Paul reached into that window and swooped up Paul unto Himself. A broken, hurting heart calls unto God like nothing else. Although no one else may see it or hear it, and it goes unnoticed by the world, it catches God's attention more than anything else, and moves Him.

Notes

Chapter 2......*Heavenly Visitation*, by Kevin Zadai
Xulon Press, Page 63

Chapter 16....... *The Final Quest,* by Rick Joyner
copyright 1996, Used by permission,
www.morningstarministries.org
pages-79-80

Chapter 20.........*Intra Muros* by Rebecca Springer
David C. Cook publication Elgin, Illinois
 pages14-15   94,95,96,97

Chapter............*Revealing Heaven,* by Kat Kerr
Xulon Press   pages60-61

Other Books by Summer McClellan

The Impossible Marriage

Faith What is It?

Jesus is Our Example

www.ingramcontent.com/pod-product-compliance
Lightning Source LLC
LaVergne TN
LVHW011353080426
835511LV00005B/268